THE SYSTEMS-THINKING
VISIONARY

The Systems-Thinking Visionary

How to Blend Big-Picture Thinking with Laser-Focus Execution

Michael G. Walker

Published by Game Changer Publishing

Paperback ISBN: 978-1-966659-91-4

Hardcover ISBN: 978-1-966659-92-1

Digital ISBN: 978-1-966659-93-8

DEDICATION

To the Visionaries who build, who dare...
who make the impossible—REAL.

May these pages be the bridge between the extraordinary
vision in your mind and the reality waiting to emerge.
Because the world doesn't need more dreamers...
It needs more doers.

All In,
MGW

READ THIS FIRST

Just to say thanks for buying and reading my book, I would like to give you a few free bonus gifts, no strings attached.

Download Your Free Gifts Now:

THE SYSTEMS-THINKING VISIONARY

HOW TO BLEND BIG-PICTURE THINKING WITH LASER-FOCUS EXECUTION

MICHAEL G. WALKER

ACKNOWLEDGMENTS

"Mike Walker's approach to business is a game-changer for anyone looking to master the art of systems thinking. His ability to break down complex ideas into actionable insights makes his work an invaluable resource for consultants, business leaders, and problem-solvers alike. I have personally had the benefit of Mike's expertise and cannot speak highly enough of his talent, passion, and integrity. He offers practical strategies to navigate and optimize intricate systems. A must-follow for those ready to elevate their business, mindset, and results!"

—Jackie Woodside | CPC, MSW. NY Times Best Selling Author, Human Potential Trainer

"Working with Mike was transformational for our company during an extremely fragile period. When I was confronted with an existential threat back in April, the way he deftly managed that transition while also handling my stress was remarkable. His execution has been so exceptional that we're now poised to take our business to the next level. The landscape has completely changed for us since bringing Mike on board. We're no longer in that vulnerable position we were in when we started working together. Looking back at all the critical choices I've made to move our business forward, choosing to work with Mike will always remain at the top of that list."

—Paul Graff | CEO. Healthy Young Minds

"Mike Walker supercharged my business success. He doesn't just talk about amplifying and monetizing your message—he actually delivers. After working with many so-called marketing 'experts,' Mike was the one who finally positioned me to dominate my industry. He's one of my secret weapons, and I can't recommend him highly enough."

—Byron Rodgers | CEO Bravo Research Group

"Mike Walker is the operational genius every visionary needs. While I'm dreaming big (and losing focus), he's the one making sure I am taking the next best and correct step. He has consulted with me on offers, ads, teams, and mindset. And, he's one of the best humans I know—he's genuinely invested in seeing others win."

—Tasha Blasi | Fertility and IVF Consultant

"When it came time to add automation to my business, I am so grateful I found Michael to walk me through all the nooks and crannies, as well as the big picture of what that entails. On the first phone call with him, I knew I was in the hands of someone who had expertise, and in two short months, he has gone above and beyond to make sure I have what I need to excel and expand my business. I would highly recommend him to any business owner in my scenario—seeing business success but ready for the next level."

—Kim O'Hara | Book Coach to Best Sellers

"Michael has been instrumental in the exponential growth of my business. His mentoring and upper-level strategy has transformed my business into an agile and focused machine. If you've ever struggled with applying your subject matter expertise into a business venture, Michael is your man. Best business decision I ever made."

—Yousef Badou | Founder. Emergence LLC

"Mike and the Wealthy Consultant team have completely transformed both my life and my business. Their expertise and support have streamlined my operations, increased efficiency, and unlocked new levels of growth I never thought possible. I can't imagine what my business would be like without his guidance and expertise."

—**Iggy Odighizuwa | CEO. Charlie.ai**

"Mike has a real skill in helping visionaries create processes for transferring their expertise to their clients & those around them. Client Success is very important to us at AdOutreach & Mike has helped to share unique ways to better empower our clients to succeed."

—**Aleric Heck | CEO AdOutreach**

"Mike has a crazy ability to simplify all the complex pieces of growing a business - from operations to what it takes to keep clients happy. Personally, he's been a game changer in bringing clarity to what felt insurmountable. If you're serious about having a healthy business, absorb everything you can from him."

—**Josh Orr | Founder. Capital Commerce**

"Mike Walker is a straight-up genius when it comes to business... both in how to run it and how to become the kind of person who can lead at the highest level. He has this rare ability to drop one-liners that stop you in your tracks and completely shift the way you think. Anytime I'm hiring or looking for someone to elevate my business, I find myself thinking, 'I need a Mike Walker.' If you have the chance to learn from him, take it. Your business will never be the same."

—**Marley Jaxx | CEO Jaxx Productions**

FOREWORD
BY TAYLOR WELCH

It is rare to find a framework that *works* these days.

Most prolific business builders find more fulfillment in *building* than they do in teaching and explaining their work, making it difficult to figure out *what* they're doing (let alone how). When I find something that has been tested, validated, and proven, I get excited.

Entrepreneurs and visionaries are fond of learning things the hard way. We are a crazy bunch. Although we wouldn't label it the "hard way," learning through the storm of trial and error is most definitely the hardest way to do it.

Years ago, when I started my very first brand, I was 100% convinced that it would be easy and all I had to do was get started. There was a wind in my sails, and everything felt worth the effort. But as things got bigger, the fatigue started to wear on me. There is a mental fatigue, a physical fatigue, and an *emotional* fatigue. Physical fatigue is easy to identify, and it just means you need a break. Mental fatigue is harder to spot and shows up in the form of confusion and overwhelm. When your brain stops working and even the simplest of decisions become existential, you're experiencing mental fatigue.

But the worst of them is emotional fatigue.

For several years, I plowed through system after system. I was stubborn, like most of us are, and convinced that the issues I was experiencing were everyone else's fault—I just needed to find the right people! But then I'd burn them out, or they'd quit. It took many years to realize that *I*, not them, was the crazy one!

Visionaries tend to jump first and figure it out later.

We can run at a pace that does not make sense, fueled by adrenaline, high aspirations, and *VISION!* But unless we break that vision down into palatable pieces, nobody will follow us or help make those visions a reality.

What Mike does so well is what very few people can do: creating systems to expand your capacity for vision *while* increasing your odds of success. The bigger the vision is, the more inspiring it will be. The smaller you can break the vision down, the easier it will be to accomplish.

When I started working with Mike, I told him that I wanted to change the world. Not only was he on board, he took my vision and made it even bigger. But as I watched him work, I noticed something peculiar. He had a unique ability to make the vision *plain* and systematize it around targets so that more people could *buy into* it.

Today, all of our organizations, on some level, run on a system that Mike has built or helped create. There is no one in the world I trust more when it comes to creating *repeatable*, step-by-step containers to house BIG, world-changing projects.

If you read this book, scratch that—if you *study* it and *practice* it —you will produce a noticeable lift in your ability to create FOLLOW-THROUGH as a visionary. This book is the connective tissue between us visionaries and the people who help us create change. And it's written by someone I trust very much. I hope you not only enjoy the book, but *engage* the book actively as you move the world through your work.

The only way to fly higher is to take people with you who can fly with you.

This book is a manual for how to do that well.

CONTENTS

INTRODUCTION

The email hit my inbox at 2:47 a.m.:

"Mike, I'm watching everything I built crumble. We scaled too fast, the systems are breaking, my team is burnt out, and I've lost sight of why I started this in the first place. I don't know how much longer I can keep going..."

Another visionary leader on the brink of collapse. A story I've seen play out time and time again—brilliant entrepreneurs with world-changing ideas who hit an invisible wall. Their companies grow, their influence expands, but something fundamental starts to break down.

The saddest part about this is that it's entirely preventable.

The tragedy isn't just the business failure. It's the cost of unrealized visions. Every time a visionary leader crashes and burns, the world loses something precious—innovations that could have transformed industries, solutions that could have solved pressing problems, and breakthroughs that could have improved countless lives.

I know because I've been there. Fourteen years ago, I was that entrepreneur—driven by big dreams but drowning in complexity.

My business was growing, but I was working 80-hour weeks, missing my daughter's dance recitals, and slowly losing my grip on the very vision that had inspired me to start my journey in the first place.

From the outside looking in, most would likely assume my company hit the wall because the vision outpaced our team's ability to execute, or we simply didn't push hard enough. The truth? I had the vision of a Tesla but was running on the operating system of a Model T. It wasn't about me needing to work harder or dream bigger —it was because there was a fundamental mismatch between my aspirations as the founder and the infrastructure of the business.

Over time, I learned a painful lesson:

"Being the owner of a dream does not, by default, grant the license or the ability to bring it to fruition."

This realization led me on a quest to bridge the gap between visionary thinking and systems thinking—two ways of operating that most people consider opposites. But what I discovered ended up revolutionizing the way I ran my business and my entire paradigm of what it meant to be a leader. More importantly, though, it revealed a pathway that any visionary leader can follow to turn their boldest dreams into reality.

In the pages ahead, I'm going to share everything I've learned about being what I call a "Systems-Thinking Visionary"—a leader who can see both the forest *and* the trees, who can dream big while building smart, who can scale without losing their soul.

Inside these pages, you'll discover:

- Why most visionaries hit a ceiling (and how to break through it)
- How to build systems that amplify rather than constrain your vision
- The quantum approach to decision-making that will transform how you lead

- Why traditional leadership advice fails visionary leaders (and what to do instead)
- How to scale your impact without sacrificing your purpose

But let me be clear—this isn't just another "business book" to consume once and then place on the shelf to collect dust. This is a blueprint for transformation. Whether you're leading a startup or a Fortune 500 company, disrupting industries, or building something entirely new, the principles in this book have the capacity to fundamentally change how you bring your vision to life.

The world doesn't need more visionaries who burn bright and fade fast. It needs visionary leaders who can build lasting engines of impact. It needs dreamers who can also be builders. It needs you to master both the art of vision and the science of systems.

That's exactly what this book will help you do.

So, if you're ready to transcend the limitations that hold most visionaries back...

If you're committed to adopting a new paradigm for making your boldest dreams a reality...

If you want to build something that outlasts you...

Your journey to becoming a Systems-Thinking Visionary starts with understanding exactly *how* to get the most from this book—how to turn these pages into a practical roadmap for transformation.

PURPOSE & FUNCTION

"Every visionary who changed the world had one thing in common—they weren't just dreamers who could see the future, they were architects who could build it."

So, are you just a visionary?
Or are you also a builder?

You've probably heard the saying "Knowledge is Power" more times than you can count. Well, here's the thing—that's only half true. Don't get me wrong, knowledge is incredibly valuable, but it's only *potential* power, it's not the whole story.

Over the years, I've met plenty of brilliant folks whose heads are crammed full of information, but they're not seeing any real success. Why? Because knowing stuff is just the starting point. The world only benefits when you take that knowledge and actually *do something with it.*

The fact that you picked up this book with the word "systems" in the title tells me you get that. You're not just here to fill your brain with more insights and facts; you're looking to turn information into real-world results. And that's exactly what this book is all about. I'm going to share with you everything I've learned from over 20+ years of being in the trenches, working with businesses of all shapes and sizes.

As you move through these pages, you'll find that each chapter serves as a practical guide, not just a bunch of theory. We're going to roll up our sleeves and get into the nitty-gritty of how to actually apply this stuff. At the end of each chapter, you'll find questions designed to help you internalize what we've covered and figure out exactly how to make it work for your unique situation.

Write (or draw) in the margins, highlight, transcribe, earmark the pages... whatever you need to do to extract and apply the actionable methodologies we're going to cover. Remember, the real value isn't simply in what you learn, it's in what you do with what you learn. As a mentor once told me, "Mike, turning knowledge into power is a deliberate process. It takes reflection, application, and constant fine-tuning." I couldn't have said it better myself.

So with the foundation in place, let's get into what it truly means to be a Systems-Thinking Visionary. Right out of the gates, Chapter 1 will challenge everything you think you know about leadership and open your eyes to possibilities you might never have considered.

We've got a lot of ground to cover, and even more to achieve.

Let's go.

ONE
UNLOCKING YOUR VISIONARY POTENTIAL

TOPIC: DEMYSTIFYING SYSTEMS THINKING

"To know thyself is the beginning of wisdom."
—Socrates

DEMYSTIFYING SYSTEMS-THINKING

In business circles, the term "visionary" gets tossed around a lot—like confetti at a New Year's party. But if you ask ten people, I'll bet my bottom dollar you'll get ten different answers.

In fact, as an experiment while writing this manuscript, I reached out to a cross-section of clients and asked what being a visionary meant to them. Below are their responses. Maybe you can relate to some of them? What comes to mind for you?

"The ability to shift someone's worldview."
–Marcia Schaefer

"Predicting the future by creating it."
–Gonzalo Hurtado

"It means accepting that you don't have to be the f**ing operator and do ALL the things."
–Ben Brickweg

"Responsibility + Creativity + Problem Solver."
–Stephanie Crassweller

"Seeing the future clearly as if it's happening today."
–David Stancin

"Designing a future reality you believe in."
–Varti Deuchoghlian

"Being naturally anchored in the future, seeing the reality of
what's possible, needed, and exciting."
–Michael McGreey

"It's bringing the vision you have for the future to life and
seeing it with your own eyes. Taking the intangible and
making it tangible for yourself & others."
–Corey McDaniel

"The ability to live into the future you envision with so
much energy and force that you create a vacuum that pulls
the right people with you to create more velocity towards
that future."
–Kelly Castor

"Having the ability to listen, trust, and follow God on your
path that He has set out for you, no matter whether it looks
like things are falling apart or flowing along."
–Tanya Williams

"Someone who has the ability to call in their wildest desires without needing to know the how."
–Stephanie Wigner

"A visionary isn't just a person who can see the long-term plans of the company, they are the person that communicates those plans in a way that inspires others and creates alignment with the company."
–Adam Kifer

"I believe that true visionaries live life inside of a single question: How can I make the world work for 100% of humanity, 100% of the time, without damaging the environment or harming people."
–Brody Lee

"Visionary $\rightarrow$ Creating a future for yourself without limitations/barriers... while knowing it all works out in the end!"
–Richard Gibbons

"Someone who can create a reality where the present moment gravitationally pulls in a wild and unknown future, while inspiring others to help bring it to life."
–Edward Stranks

"A "visionary" is a feeler, believer, and DREAMER. A "visionary *armed with* Systems Thinking" is a legend, deliverer, and LEGACY-MAKER."
–Bijal Patel

"Shaping reality to meet the potential you can see more clearly than anyone else."
–Aleric Heck

"An immature visionary is someone who succumbs to the vision, chaos, and seduction of their opportunistic energy. A mature visionary is someone who channels their chaotic nature to realize their genius with an undying and obsessive focus on victory."
—JonCameron Johnson

Don't you find it interesting that we can all use the same word to describe someone and yet it can mean such a wide variety of things to different people? As simple as this may first appear on the surface, this seemingly mundane variation in definition has significant ramifications, especially in the world of business.

This isn't just semantics. These variations in how we define and understand leadership roles create real-world friction that can cost businesses millions. Think about it: When a founder says they want a "visionary CMO" but hasn't clearly defined what that means, they'll likely hire someone whose definition doesn't match theirs. When a client engages you as a "visionary consultant," but their interpretation differs from yours, misalignment is inevitable. The result? Wasted resources, frustrated teams, and failed initiatives.

This is why getting crystal clear on these definitions is mission-critical. When everyone in your organization shares the same understanding of what it means to be a visionary leader, alignment becomes natural rather than forced. Your systems, your team, and your results all flow from this fundamental clarity.

That said, let's get crystal clear on what being a Systems-Thinking Visionary means before we venture into the coming chapters together.

THE ESSENCE OF VISIONARY LEADERSHIP

For many, being a visionary is all about having some grand, pie-in-the-sky ideas or dreaming up a future that looks like it's straight out of a sci-fi flick. There may be some elements of truth in that, but in the make-or-break world of business leadership, it needs to go way deeper than that.

A visionary isn't just someone with their head in the clouds. They're the ones who can see beyond the horizon, spotting golden opportunities where others see nothing but roadblocks. They're the ones who can chart a course through the stormy seas of uncertainty with the confidence of a seasoned sea captain. Visionaries have this rare cocktail of foresight, creativity, and strategic thinking that lets them sniff out market shifts before they happen, grasp emerging trends, and envision possibilities that aren't on anyone else's radar yet.

From a high-level perspective, that's a great place to start. But what sets a true visionary leader apart isn't only their ability to daydream about the future. It's their knack for actively shaping it. They can take their vision and communicate it in a way that lights a fire under people, turning abstract ideas into concrete game plans. This ability to bridge the gap between vision and reality? That is what separates the visionary leaders from the daydreamers.

To be a true visionary leader means more than just having the creativity to imagine what could be—it's about having the discipline to map out the steps to get there, rallying the troops, and orchestrating the resources to bring that vision to life.

And let's be clear, being a visionary does not require having a crystal ball and predicting the future with 100% accuracy. It also means being flexible and resilient when the winds of change start blowing. Visionary leaders get that the path to realizing their goal is rarely a straight line. They're ready to navigate the twists and turns, adjusting their strategies on the fly without losing sight of the big picture.

In short, being a true visionary leader means being both the dreamer *and* the doer. The thinker and the integrator. It requires a deep understanding of the current landscape, coupled with the guts to challenge the status quo and the wisdom to guide others toward a future that's still taking shape.

THE VISIONARY-INTEGRATOR POLARITY

Visionary: A leader who excels at identifying future opportunities and imagining breakthrough solutions that don't yet exist. Traditionally viewed as "big picture thinkers," visionaries are known for their ability to see beyond current limitations and inspire others toward ambitious goals.

Integrator: A leader who specializes in transforming abstract concepts into executable strategies through systematic planning and implementation. Typically recognized as "detail-oriented problem solvers," integrators create the operational frameworks that bring ideas to life.

While these definitions reflect how most organizations view these roles, this traditional separation has created an artificial barrier that limits visionary leaders' true potential.

If you've been in the business game for even a hot minute, and especially if you've had to wrangle teams, you've no doubt run into these two seemingly opposite styles of thinking that pop up in the human chess game of management and leadership.

There's no shortage of books and content out there harping on about the differences between visionary and systems thinkers. And yeah, they are different beasts to be sure. You might've even found yourself scratching your head, trying to figure out how to get your ideas across to someone on your team when it feels like you're speaking totally different languages.

Quick side note for all you leaders out there: Just because we're talking doesn't mean we're actually communicating. (We'll dive deeper into that in Chapter 7.)

There are definitely traits and quirks that stand out in both these archetypes. But here's where I'm going to ruffle some feathers—I don't buy that you have to be either a visionary *or* a systems person. It's not an either/or situation. While we might naturally lean one way or the other, I'm proposing the idea that *we can actually be both*.

By nurturing this belief, we can accomplish much more, way more efficiently, and lead people with a whole new level of impact. Yes, you heard me right. I believe it's not only possible but downright preferable to be a Systems-Thinking Visionary. That's why I named the book the way I did. It's more than just a catchy title—it's a whole new way of running an organization.

Think of this concept as the latest software upgrade for your brain. My goal with this book is to rewire how you see yourself and your business. To show you that being a dreamer and an integrator aren't mutually exclusive. But to pull this off, you've got to be willing to unsubscribe from old ways of doing things that are no longer serving you and learn some new ways of processing and disseminating information. And just like anything new, it might feel a bit uncomfortable at first. (In fact, I'll go so far as to say that if it doesn't, you're probably not pushing yourself hard enough.)

We all have our natural-born gifts and strengths—they're the bedrock of our success as leaders. But we can't shy away from expanding on those and stepping into our weak spots. It's like going to the gym—it's only when we push against resistance that our muscles grow stronger.

To do this effectively, though, we'll need to stop hiding behind old beliefs that are holding us back. One such belief is that visionary leaders should stick to the big ideas and leave all the nitty-gritty execution stuff to the integrators. You know those phrases like "I'm just the idea person" or "That's for the operations team to figure out." These kinds of statements create a false divide between vision and execution, and they undermine a leader's responsibility to make sure their ideas translate into actionable plans.

When visionary leaders distance themselves from systems and operational tasks, they risk losing touch with how their vision is being interpreted and implemented. This can lead to a disconnect between the high-level strategy and the day-to-day grind, leaving teams struggling with unclear expectations or objectives that are out of whack with what's actually happening out on the front lines of the business. The idea that "details will sort themselves out" or that "someone else will make it work" can create a culture where leaders duck accountability for the execution phase, which is absolutely crucial for turning visionary ideas into real-world results.

By embracing systems thinking, visionary leaders can get their hands dirty with the processes that allow their ideas to thrive, making sure both creativity and operational excellence are firing on all cylinders for sustainable success, while at the same time avoiding getting mired down in the weeds of detail that traps their creativity and working on high-leverage solutions.

Ask most successful entrepreneurs about their role models, and you'll hear names like Steve Jobs, Elon Musk, or Richard Branson. We celebrate these visionaries for their bold ideas and revolutionary thinking. But here's what most people miss—these leaders didn't just dream up ideas and hand them off to others to figure out. They were deeply involved in the systems and processes that brought their visions to life.

Take Steve Jobs. Everyone knows him as the visionary behind Apple's revolutionary products. But what many don't realize is that Jobs was obsessed with operational details from the exact curve of a product's edges to the specific steps in the customer experience at Apple stores. He wasn't just "the idea guy," he was neck-deep in the systems that turned those ideas into reality.

The dangerous myth in business today is that visionary leaders should float above the details, focusing solely on the "what" while leaving the "how" to others. This hands-off approach has led countless promising companies to fail, not because their vision was wrong, but because their leaders never bridged the gap between imagination and implementation.

The hard truth? *Your brilliant ideas are worthless if you can't speak the language of execution.* Your team can't build what they can't understand, and they can't understand what you won't take the time to properly architect.

So, while there are definitely visionaries and integrators out there with their unique strengths, I'm challenging every leader, regardless of their default mode of thinking, to consider that there are massive advantages to learning the other language. You CAN be both, without sacrificing your passion for big-picture problem-solving, and in doing so, you'll become a far more impactful leader—one who not only dreams big dreams but backs them up with clearly defined plans of achievement.

BLIND SPOTS

Now that we've nailed down what true visionary leadership is really all about—its nature and boundaries—it's just as crucial to shine a light on the challenges that come with this unique mindset. By addressing these blindspots head-on, we can sidestep potential pitfalls and shore them up with insights and support from people, habits, and systems.

As we covered earlier, visionary leaders often have this uncanny ability to see beyond the horizon, imagining a future that others can't even fathom yet. They dream big, think bold, and inspire those around them to push past their limits. But this extraordinary gift comes with its own set of hurdles. And if we're not careful, these obstacles can trip up even the most brilliant minds.

Picture your mind as a multimillion-dollar supercar, capable of mind-blowing speed, handling, and power. But without knowing how to harness that power properly, its potential is not only wasted, it can become downright dangerous. There is, after all, such a thing as too much power when it's not paired with precision and control.

This is where a lot of would-be great leaders stumble. Their supercharged brains, brimming with creativity and potential, can sometimes overwhelm their ability to direct that energy with laser-like focus. As a result, their immense potential scatters like loose papers in a windstorm, leaving a trail of unrealized dreams.

While the variables and nuances are too numerous to list in their entirety, my experience has shown that there are a handful of common challenges that most visionaries face. I call these the **Five Opposing Forces of Visionary Leadership**.

The most dangerous traps are the ones we don't know we're in, and the hardest foes to conquer are the ones we can't see. These forces often lurk in the shadows of our ambitions, subtly undermining our progress. But by dragging them into the light, we can sidestep unnecessary complexity and navigate around them with a state of flow that only comes from self-awareness. Recognizing that we have blind spots isn't a sign of weakness, it's a strategic advantage. By acknowledging these handicaps for what they are, we drastically reduce their ability to hold us back from our God-given calling.

THE FIVE OPPOSING FORCES OF VISIONARY LEADERSHIP

Over the years of working with clients across dozens of industries, I've spotted five recurring obstacles. These forces, if left unchecked, can turn a visionary's greatest strengths into liabilities. By getting a handle on these forces and tackling them head-on, leaders can better harness their full potential to transform their visions into reality.

As you consider each of these forces, I want you to reflect on your journey so far. Do any of these ring a bell? Have they shown up in your past experiences, or do you see them lurking in your current challenges? If so, don't freak out—recognition is the first step to mastery. Take note of the forces that speak to you because, in the chapters ahead, we're going to dig into practical solutions and strategies to conquer these forces, empowering you to lead with clarity, precision, and impact.

Force 1: Action Void

Visionaries often knock it out of the park when it comes to generating big ideas. After all, that's usually their zone of genius, but the real challenge kicks in when it's time to turn those ideas into reality. The Action Void represents that gap between *inspiration* and *realization,* where brilliant concepts can stall out due to a lack of actionable steps. This force shows up as a sense of stagnation, where leaders might feel stuck in the idea phase without a clear roadmap on how to move forward.

It's like standing on the edge of a deep valley with a breathtaking view of possibilities on the other side, but not being able to cross to reach them. This void can be particularly frustrating because the visionary can see the end goal with total clarity, but the steps to get there are buried beneath the weight of logistics, namely **Provisions** (resources, knowledge), **People** (team, mentorship), and **Process** (reliable methods). It's a space where ideas, no matter how groundbreaking, risk sinking into oblivion under the weight of moving parts. If left unchecked, visionaries might find themselves endlessly refining concepts, seeking perfection before taking action, or simply giving up due to being overwhelmed by the enormity of their vision.

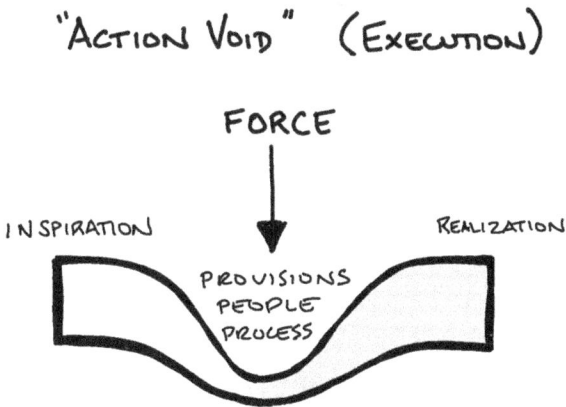

"ACTION VOID" (EXECUTION)

FORCE

INSPIRATION   REALIZATION

PROVISIONS
PEOPLE
PROCESS

Throughout history, even the most brilliant minds have wrestled with this force. Take Thomas Edison, who famously said, "Genius is 1% inspiration and 99% perspiration." Edison's success didn't come solely from his ability to envision what could be, it came from his relentless commitment to bridging the gap between inspiration and realization. He understood that ideas are only as valuable as the effort invested in bringing them to life.

The Action Void can be overcome, but it requires a deliberate strategy that breaks down grand visions into smaller, manageable tasks that steadily build toward the larger goal. Throughout this book, we'll cover several actionable strategies to address this force.

Force 2: Ambition Overload

Ambition is the rocket fuel of visionaries, propelling them to reach beyond the ordinary and aim for extraordinary achievements. But when ambition isn't balanced with sustainability, it can quickly become a double-edged sword.

Ambition Overload kicks in when the relentless pursuit of goals outpaces our capacity to sustain that drive, resulting in depleted *Energy*, *Money*, and *Time*. This force can show up in opposing ways. Most people are familiar with the term burnout, or what I call "red-lining," but it often shows up first as a creeping sense of low energy, where the weight of countless objectives and sky-high expectations begins to crush the very spirit that once fueled the passion.

Ambition Overload is like a powerful engine running at full throttle without pause—eventually, even the strongest machine will overheat and break down. Visionaries, driven by their desire to achieve greatness, can sometimes lose sight of their limitations and the needs of those around them. The result isn't just personal exhaustion but also the risk of burning out your team, leading to a nosedive in morale, productivity, and overall effectiveness. The once-clear vision becomes clouded by total fatigue or is replaced by a sense of lukewarm obligation rather than peak-state inspiration.

Identifying these warning signs early is a skill worth cultivating.

Like the red warning light on a car's dashboard, they are signals of unseen issues that, if caught early enough, can prevent total mechanical breakdown. We'll dive deeper into this in the coming chapters.

"AMBITION OVERLOAD" (FUEL)

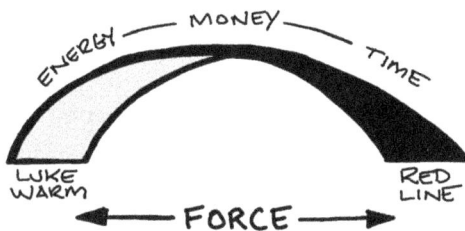

ENERGY — MONEY — TIME

LUKE WARM   RED LINE

◄— FORCE —►

Force 3: Signal Loss

Translating visionary ideas into actionable, understandable concepts can be a real head-scratcher, especially when those ideas need to be executed by a diverse team. Visionaries often assume that their enthusiasm and clarity of thought will naturally transfer to others, but this assumption usually leads to some major misunderstandings. George Bernard Shaw, who won the Nobel Prize for Literature, nailed it when he said, "The single biggest problem in communication is the illusion that it has taken place." It's a powerful reminder that communication isn't just about speaking; it's about ensuring that the message is actually understood and internalized by those who receive it.

Signal Loss happens when there's a disconnect between the visionary's intent and the team's interpretation. This force can show up in subtle ways: a nod of agreement that masks confusion or a project that veers off course because team members moved on instructions differently than intended. The result is misalignment, where the outcome falls short of the original vision, leading to frustration and missed opportunities. Leaders need to recognize that communication is a two-way street, requiring not only clarity in delivery but also active engagement to confirm that the message has been accurately received and understood.

As visionary leaders, we often have this impulse to talk; we associate oration with "leadership," which it certainly can be. But we can't neglect the necessity (and effectiveness) of collecting input and feedback from those we trust to provide it.

Here's a somewhat funny quip that I picked up somewhere along the way and that I often share with clients: God gave us two ears and one mouth, and we should use them in that same ratio (meaning we should listen twice as much as we talk). In Chapter 7, we'll discuss simple and effective ways of soliciting feedback to ensure clarity and resonance with your team.

The importance of this concept carries even more weight within large organizations where various teams may become siloed within the operation and plans of their individual departments and lose sight of how their responsibilities fit within the larger vision of the organization. As a leader, never just assume that your team sees what you see. Resolving this Signal Loss means first *Envisioning* the desired outcome, *Inspiring* change through understanding, *Inviting* your team to buy into the mission, and then *Engaging* in the steps necessary to accomplish the goal with total clarity and focus.

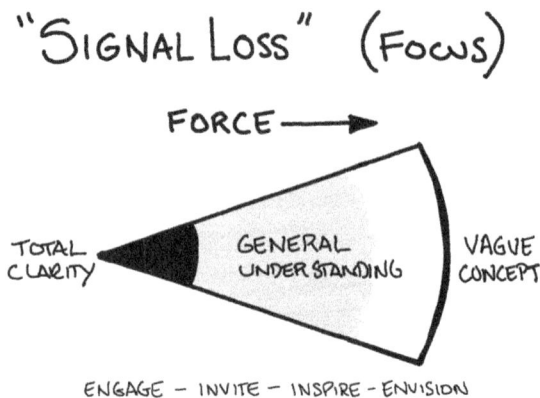

"SIGNAL LOSS" (FOCUS)

FORCE →

TOTAL CLARITY — GENERAL UNDERSTANDING — VAGUE CONCEPT

ENGAGE — INVITE — INSPIRE — ENVISION

Force 4: Change Drag

Visionaries are natural agents of change; they typically thrive on it and seek it out like a vampire does for blood. But resistance to change is an inevitable force they often face. Change Drag is the friction encountered when implementing new ideas or driving transformation within an organization. This resistance can come from entrenched habits, red tape within bureaucratic environments, outdated mindsets, or even fear of the unknown, slowing down progress and causing frustration.

This can be particularly painful in the area of hiring and firing of team members where some people may not grow professionally at the same rate as the needs of the organization. Truth be told, the team that got you "here" may not be the same one who gets you "there."

Galileo Galilei, the brilliant 17th-century astronomer and physicist who challenged the widely accepted belief that the Earth was the center of the universe, experienced this force firsthand and almost lost his life because of it. Galileo's visionary work, which supported the Copernican theory that the Earth and other planets revolved around the Sun, sparked a revolution in science. Yet, despite the clarity of his observations, Galileo faced intense resistance. The established Church, which held great influence over societal beliefs, saw his ideas as a direct threat to the existing order. The resistance was so powerful that Galileo was tried by the Inquisition, forced to recant his views, and spent the rest of his life under house arrest.

Galileo's story is a potent example of Change Drag at its most severe—a visionary leader attempting to introduce groundbreaking ideas, only to be met with institutional inertia and fear of disruption. The friction Galileo faced didn't just slow his progress; it nearly silenced his voice. His story highlights a critical truth for modern leaders: change is often met with pushback, not because the new ideas are flawed, but because they challenge the comfort of the status quo.

In today's organizations, Change Drag can manifest in more

subtle but equally obstructive ways. It might appear as passive resistance from team members who are comfortable with existing processes, or as skepticism from stakeholders who are wary of venturing into uncharted territory. This force slows the pace of innovation and can also erode morale and diminish the overall effectiveness of leadership if not properly addressed.

This kind of force can certainly be stressful, but we can ease our visionary minds by simply acknowledging and accepting that resistance to change is a natural part of the human condition. As visionaries, we often view the unknown as a realm of opportunity, but for many, change equates to risk, which can trigger a cascade of emotional responses within a team. It's crucial to understand that these reactions are seldom a reflection of our ideas being undervalued or unwanted; rather, they stem from deeply ingrained paradigms that require time to adapt to new realities.

The best path forward is to anticipate and embrace this as an inherent aspect of leadership. Forge strong alliances with key stakeholders, present compelling evidence of your vision's benefits, and proactively address concerns to facilitate smoother transitions. Remember, it's natural for some team members to need more time to adjust to changes in direction.

A word of caution here: if your team lacks individuals who challenge your vision or at least ask for the rationale behind decisions, you may be surrounded by "yes men" or "yes women," people who aren't empowered or willing to question visionary ideas. This is a dangerous dynamic. While a divisive culture is undesirable, the opposite—a culture of unquestioning compliance—can be equally, if not more, dangerous. As leaders, we must encourage and cultivate an environment where team members feel safe to voice their concerns. Those who take a more conservative approach to decision-making are invaluable assets that should be nurtured.

Understanding that resistance is a natural part of the change process is the first step in overcoming it. Learning how to make new ideas feel *Relatable* is key within groups that are deeply entrenched in the status quo. In organizations that are more adaptive and open to change, the focus shifts toward the **Reliability** of the leader, which instills trust and "buy-in" from the team. In times of radical growth and change, all ideas need to be run through the filter of **Reality** to ensure that our visionary ideas don't drive the organization off the cliff in the process. By anticipating and preparing for this resistance force, we can develop strategies to engage and align our teams, turning friction into fuel for progress. We'll cover this in more detail in Chapter 3: Transforming Big Ideas Into Tangible Results.

"CHANGE DRAG" (COMMITMENT)

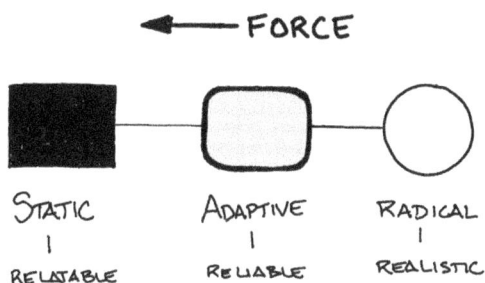

←— FORCE

STATIC   ADAPTIVE   RADICAL
| | |
RELATABLE   RELIABLE   REALISTIC

Force 5: Reality Split

As emphasized earlier, the world does not reward ideas alone—it rewards results. And those results typically emerge from ideas that are grounded in reality, validated through measurement, and proven in practice.

The journey from a groundbreaking idea to successful execution is rarely straightforward. It's not uncommon for visionaries to become so enamored with their grand visions that they overlook the practical constraints that inevitably arise—whether it's limited resources, time, or team capabilities. Reality Split occurs when lofty aspirations collide with the practical limitations of the real world. This opposing force between **Control** and **Variables** often requires a recalibration of expectations.

Take, for instance, the story of the Concorde, the supersonic passenger jet that promised to revolutionize air travel by drastically reducing flight times. The vision was bold and inspiring, capturing the imagination of both the public and industry leaders. However, as the project progressed, the realities of fuel costs, environmental concerns, and noise regulations began to weigh heavily on its success. Despite the groundbreaking technology and the initial excitement, the Concorde was eventually retired due to its unsustainable operating costs and limited market appeal.

The Concorde's story is a classic example of Reality Split. What began as an audacious vision ultimately had to be tempered by the practical realities of economics and infrastructure. For visionary leaders, the lesson is clear: while "big thinking" is crucial, it must be balanced with a keen understanding of the limitations and constraints involved. The ability to adapt and refine your goals in response to these realities is what differentiates a fleeting idea from a sustainable achievement.

This force underscores the importance of adaptability and pragmatism in leadership. It's not enough to simply set ambitious goals; those goals must be *Measurable, Achievable, Valuable*, and *Adaptable*. Leaders who recognize and navigate Reality Split are better positioned to turn their visions into lasting success, rather than seeing them fizzle out in the face of insurmountable challenges. Naturally, having people on your team with complementary and even opposing skill sets can be incredibly useful. We don't know what we don't know. This is where blending the right team with disciplined and decisive decision-making becomes paramount—a topic we'll look closely at in Chapter 6: Quantum Decision-Making.

"Reality Split" (Complexity)

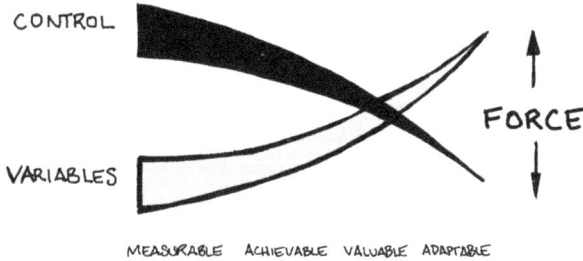

QUESTIONS TO CONSIDER

1. Are your big ideas consistently turning into actionable plans, or do they often remain just ideas without a clear path forward? (We'll discuss this further in Chapter 3.)

2. Do those around you fully grasp your vision, or do you often find that your ideas lose clarity as they're communicated?

3. Are you managing your drive in a way that's sustainable, or are you pushing yourself and your team to the point of burnout?

4. Have you taken the time to consider the early indicators of burnout?

5. Are you encountering resistance when driving change, and how effectively are you transforming that resistance into momentum?

6. Are your goals aligned with the realities of your resources and capabilities, or do you find yourself needing to frequently adjust your plans?

7. When you reflect on the Five Opposing Forces of Visionary Leadership, which one resonates most strongly with your current challenges? What specific systems could you implement to address it?

The questions at the end of each chapter aren't meant to be answered once and forgotten. They're guideposts for your ongoing journey of visionary leadership. Revisit them regularly, especially as you hit new stages of growth or face significant decisions.

As you reflect on these questions, you might be wondering how to actually implement these ideas in practice. This is where systems thinking becomes crucial. In Chapter 2, we'll explore how to create frameworks that turn inspiring visions into operational reality.

Before we go any further, invest a couple of minutes to download the tools and resources that we'll refer to as we move through the chapters. This will help you get the most actionable leverage from investing your time going through these pages. You can access them free at: SystemsThinkingVisionary.com/resources.

TWO
THE POWER GRID FRAMEWORK
TOPIC: REVOLUTIONIZING HOW TO
APPROACH BUSINESS PROBLEMS

"The most powerful tool we have in our toolkit
is the ability to create systems that work for us."
—Chris Ducker, *Rise of the Youpreneur*

REVOLUTIONIZING HOW TO APPROACH BUSINESS PROBLEMS

Systems thinking is more than just another business buzzword—it's a fundamental shift in how we perceive and interact with the world around us. Just as we clarified what it means to be a Visionary and an Integrator, let's get crystal clear on what we mean by "systems thinking."

At its core, this approach is about perceiving the world not as a collection of isolated parts, but as an interconnected whole. It's the ability to see how each element influences the others in often unexpected ways.

Think of it this way: If we were city dwellers wanting to take a trip to the beach, the vision would be the sand and waves, the business would be the vehicle we travel in, and the map would be the strategic systems used to navigate toward our ideal day in the sun. Systems thinking is what allows us to create that map, understanding the interconnections between traffic patterns, weather conditions, and our own resources to ensure we reach our destination.

This approach enables us to grasp how changes in one component can ripple through and impact the entire system, sometimes in ways that are unexpected but highly significant. And it's this ripple effect that often catches well-meaning visionaries off guard. The second-, third-, and fourth-order consequences that can come from thinking at the macro level but not seeing deeper and downstream can be brutal.

If you've ever found yourself overwhelmed by the complexity of bringing your vision to life, you're not alone. It's these countless variables stemming from big goals that cause many would-be successful visionaries to stop before they even start—or worse, quit after years of toil.

But here's the good news that may be counterintuitive to common belief. As a visionary, *you're already hardwired for systems thinking*. You have an innate ability to see connections and possibilities that others miss. The challenge is channeling that ability into practical, actionable strategies, which is what this book is completely dedicated to helping you do!

STORYBOARDING YOUR VISION

The first step in applying systems thinking to your business is to contextualize your vision within a system framework. This involves mapping out the key components, stakeholders, and processes involved in bringing your vision to life.

"A vision without a system of implementation is just a dream. A system without a vision is just busy work. But a vision powered by a well-designed system can change the world."

Now, I know for many, the idea of mapping out schematics and flowcharts is about as fun as pouring salt in their eyes (*ouch!*). So let me ease those minds right now by saying that although you can go full-on "geek mode" when it comes to drawing out systems, you DO NOT need to go this route. In fact, even if you're like me and actually enjoy architecting graphical depictions of operational processes (yes, I'm one of "those people"), my suggestion is that you purposely start by keeping things stupid simple.

Like I tell clients all the time—brevity exposes clarity. If you can't explain a high-level overview of a system to another team member on one piece of paper, you're either going far too granular or you're simply confusing complexity with performance enhancement. In reality, unnecessary complexity just invites friction and slows things down. As Leonardo da Vinci said, "Simplicity is the ultimate sophistication."

Whether you want to simply draw on a piece of paper by hand or use any of today's online tools that support creating shapes, lines, and text, start by creating a visual representation of your business ecosystem. This could be a system diagram, a flowchart, or even a mind map. The goal is simply to illustrate the connections and dependencies between different elements of your business. At first, just illustrate this in macro terms, avoiding too much detail, but then over time, you can include everything from your team structure and operational processes to your customer touchpoints and market influences.

Here's just one very simple example. No doubt yours will look very different.

Foundation

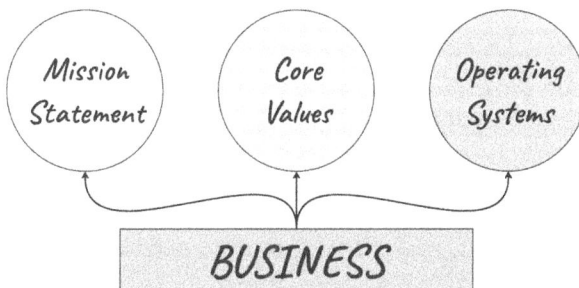

Version 1.0

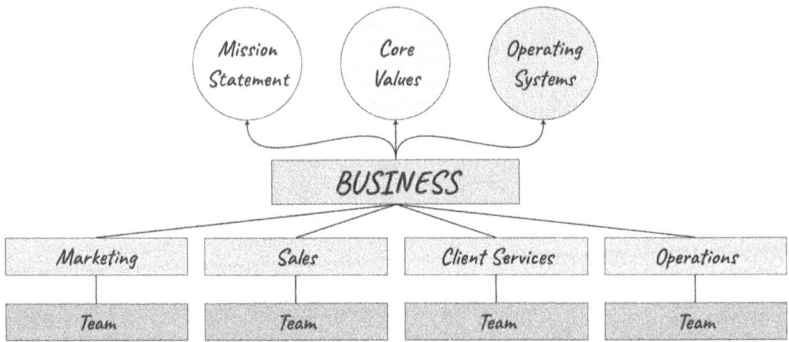

Version 2.0

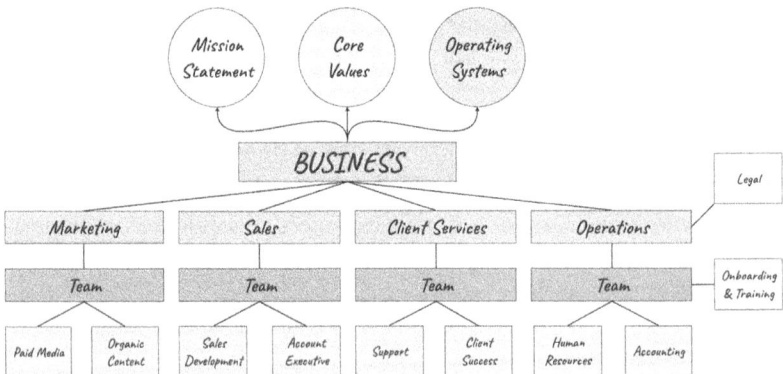

This mapping exercise serves several crucial purposes:

1. It provides a clear blueprint for action, making your vision more tangible and actionable.
2. It helps identify potential bottlenecks or weak links in your current system.
3. It reveals hidden connections that might not be apparent when viewing individual components in isolation.

Something important to remember here is that this map isn't set in stone as a once-and-done project. It's a living document that should evolve as your understanding of the system deepens and your business grows and changes. The key is to start simple and refine as you go, always keeping the big picture in mind while gradually adding the necessary details.

In fact, I'm quite confident that if you take the time to draw a simple "version 1.0" now, it'll change dramatically by the time you finish this book. Take five minutes right now to map this out (again, no perfectionism; let's keep the momentum up). But get this done now as we're going to optimize it right away in the next section.

POWER MOVES

Got that first draft in hand? Great, now that you have a high-level map of your business system, let's talk about where to focus your energy for maximum impact.

I call these strategic focus areas your "Power Moves"—essentially the highest leverage decisions and actions that create massive ripple effects throughout your entire organization. They're like acupuncture points in your business—hit them right, and you can create systemic transformation with surprisingly little force.

Think of it like a chess master planning their game. While amateur players get caught up in individual piece movements, masters focus on board control and position. They think several moves ahead, understanding how each decision creates or limits future possibilities. Your business works the same way.

Through years of studying these patterns, I've identified four distinct "zones" where your strategic decisions have the most leverage. I've mapped them out in a simple one-page layout called The Power Grid Framework™. These zones aren't isolated departments—they're interconnected parts of a dynamic system, each amplifying or diminishing the others.

Let's break down each zone:

Zone 1: Vision & Purpose

This is the core foundation for everything we do; it's about the fundamental reason your organization exists and the transformation you're trying to create in the world. Changes here ripple through everything else.

Power Moves in this zone include:

- Redefining your market category
- Amplifying your mission's reach
- Evolving your core values
- Shifting your organizational identity

Zone 2: Systems & Structure

While Vision & Purpose sets the direction, Systems & Structure determines how effectively you can move in that direction. This zone is about the invisible architecture that shapes how work gets done in your organization.

Power Moves here include:

- Team architecture
- Communication flow optimization
- Decision-making frameworks
- Resource allocation systems

Think of this zone as your organization's nervous system. When it's working well, information flows smoothly, decisions happen at the right level, and your team operates in harmony. When it's not, you get bottlenecks, confusion, and missed opportunities.

I'll share a quick story here that illustrates this perfectly. Years ago, I worked with Tom, a savvy entrepreneur who had built a rapidly growing clothing and swimwear brand. Despite having a clear vision and a talented team, they were constantly missing marketing and exposure opportunities because their decision-making process was too centralized. Every little decision had to go through Tom, creating a massive bottleneck. If he was around, things got done quickly; if he was traveling or out surfing, things slowed down until the team heard back from him.

By redesigning their Systems & Structure zone, we transformed their operation. Instead of every decision flowing up to Tom, they created clear frameworks for different types of decisions to be made at different levels. The result? Response time to market opportunities dropped from days to minutes, and team engagement soared because people finally had real autonomy.

Zone 3: Execution & Operations

This is where things really begin to tick. You can have an inspiring vision and brilliant systems, but if your day-to-day execution isn't dialed in, you're still going to struggle. This zone is about turning big ideas into consistent results.

Power Moves in this zone include:

- Performance metric design
- Process optimization
- Resource deployment
- Quality control systems

But here's where many leaders get things wrong—they *start* here, obsessing over operational efficiency before they've nailed their Vision and Systems zones. It's like trying to tune a car engine before you know what kind of race you're entering. You might get really good at something that doesn't actually matter.

Let me give you a real-world example. One of my clients a few years ago was in the e-commerce space, driving her team crazy with constant process optimization initiatives. Every week it was a new efficiency metric, a new performance target, a new software, a new reporting requirement. Her team was drowning in data and burning out fast.

When we dug into the issue, we realized she was optimizing for the wrong things because her Vision zone wasn't clear. Once we helped her get crystal clear on her company's true purpose—helping small artisans reach global markets—everything shifted. She didn't need more data; she needed fewer but higher-quality inputs. Suddenly, those same team members who were frustrated and burning out became energized because they could see how their daily work connected to a meaningful mission. At the same time, they had greater clarity on how to measure progress and, ultimately, what "success" was supposed to look like.

Zone 4: Growth & Evolution

This is the zone that separates good companies from truly great ones. It's about building in the capacity for continuous adaptation and improvement. Think of this zone as future-proofing your organization.

Power Moves here include:

- Learning systems design
- Innovation protocols
- Adaptation frameworks
- Strategic growth checkpoints

The magic of this zone is that it's self-reinforcing. When you get it right, your organization doesn't just grow larger, it optimizes and evolves. Every challenge becomes an opportunity for learning—every setback sparks innovation.

I saw this play out beautifully with Marcus, founder of a media buying agency who met with his team each quarter to analyze three simple but powerful questions:

1. What do we know now that we didn't know before?
2. How does this change what's possible?
3. What experiments should we run next?

This simple practice turned his company into a learning machine, able to spot and seize opportunities that their competitors couldn't even see. As simple as this line of questioning is, ask yourself, "When was the last time I rounded up the team and invested even 30 minutes of brainstorming around this type of thinking?"

When you begin delegating team brain power to this level of questioning, you shift from being a competitor in the marketplace to becoming a trendsetter.

INTEGRATING THE POWER GRID

When you get all four zones working together, they create a success spiral. Each zone amplifies the others, creating exponential rather than linear growth.

Your Vision & Purpose provides the direction and energy, your Systems & Structure creates the pathways for that energy to flow, your Execution & Operations turns that energy into results, and your Growth & Evolution ensures you keep getting better over time.

Like compounding interest for your business, each zone multiplies the effectiveness of the others. A 10% improvement in each zone doesn't give you 40% better results—it can give you 100% or even 1000% better results because of how they interact.

Now, I know what you might be thinking: *This sounds great, Mike, but where do I start?*

Let's break this down into practical steps you can take right away.

First, grab that system map we created earlier. Look at your business through the lens of each zone, asking yourself these critical questions:

Zone 1: Vision & Purpose Audit

- Is our current vision actually pulling us forward or just sounding good on paper?
- Are our daily decisions aligned with our stated purpose?

- Do all team members understand and feel connected to our mission?
- What bigger impact could we be making in our market? In the world?

Zone 2: Systems & Structure Review

- Does information flow freely or get stuck in bottlenecks?
- Are decisions being made at the right level?
- Where do our systems amplify or dampen our team's natural talents?
- Where are the current friction points in our operations?

Zone 3: Execution & Operations Assessment

- Are we measuring what *truly* matters or just what's easy to measure?
- Do our processes continually improve or just maintain the status quo?
- Are resources deployed where they'll have the most impact?
- How much of our team's energy goes to value creation versus firefighting?

Zone 4: Growth & Evolution Check

- How quickly do we learn from mistakes and adapt?
- What mechanisms do we have for capturing and applying insights?
- Are we built to evolve or just to maintain?
- Where are our biggest blind spots?

Once you've done this initial assessment, look for those areas where small changes could create massive positive ripples.

Here's the key, though—and this is massively important—***don't try to fix everything at once!*** That's a recipe for overwhelm and usually leads to nothing really changing. Block out 60 minutes (yes, specifically 60, 15 minutes per zone); any less, and you'll rush, any more, and you'll overthink.

Using The Power Grid Framework™ below, write out three Power Moves for each zone that, over time, can be implemented to optimize your business. Then start with the highest leverage opportunities in zone 1—that's where the foundation is. Fortify things there first, then move sequentially through zones 2, 3, and 4.

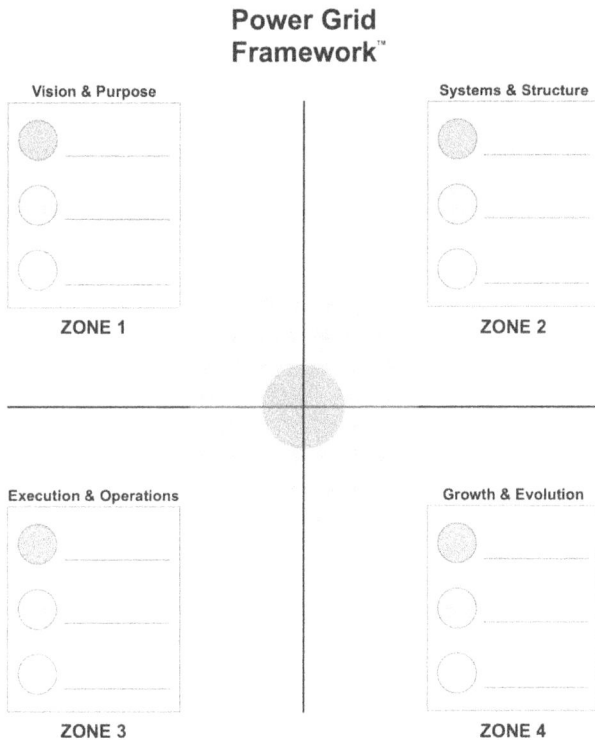

Power Grid Framework™

Vision & Purpose

ZONE 1

Systems & Structure

ZONE 2

Execution & Operations

ZONE 3

Growth & Evolution

ZONE 4

Download the PDF template at SystemsThinkingVisionary.com/resources.

Avoid perfectionism; this is about meaningful progress. Just start creating positive momentum that compounds over time. Each successful "Power Move" builds your team's confidence and capacity for the next one.

In the coming pages, we'll explore how to maintain this momentum. But first, take action on what we've covered here. The best strategy in the world means nothing without execution.

Here's a simple example of how this works in action:

Power Grid Framework™

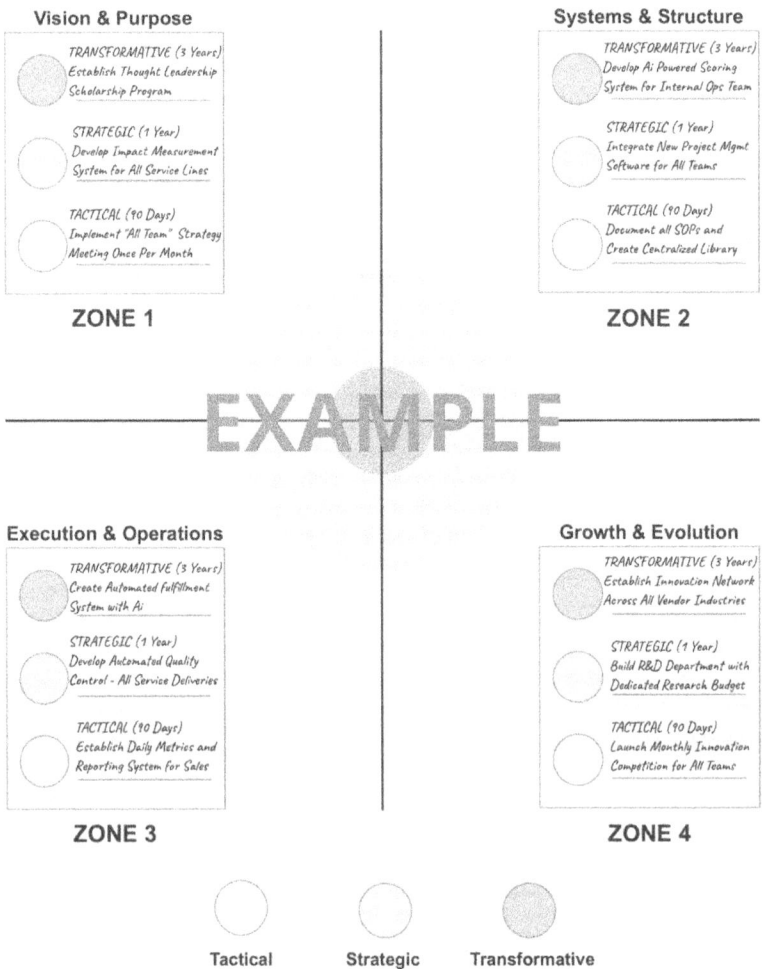

Vision & Purpose

TRANSFORMATIVE (3 Years)
Establish Thought Leadership
Scholarship Program

STRATEGIC (1 Year)
Develop Impact Measurement
System for All Service Lines

TACTICAL (90 Days)
Implement "All Team" Strategy
Meeting Once Per Month

ZONE 1

Systems & Structure

TRANSFORMATIVE (3 Years)
Develop Ai Powered Scoring
System for Internal Ops Team

STRATEGIC (1 Year)
Integrate New Project Mgmt
Software for All Teams

TACTICAL (90 Days)
Document all SOPs and
Create Centralized Library

ZONE 2

EXAMPLE

Execution & Operations

TRANSFORMATIVE (3 Years)
Create Automated Fulfillment
System with Ai

STRATEGIC (1 Year)
Develop Automated Quality
Control - All Service Deliveries

TACTICAL (90 Days)
Establish Daily Metrics and
Reporting System for Sales

ZONE 3

Growth & Evolution

TRANSFORMATIVE (3 Years)
Establish Innovation Network
Across All Vendor Industries

STRATEGIC (1 Year)
Build R&D Department with
Dedicated Research Budget

TACTICAL (90 Days)
Launch Monthly Innovation
Competition for All Teams

ZONE 4

Tactical   Strategic   Transformative

© The Systems Thinking Visionary

INSTALLING FEEDBACK LOOPS

Feedback loops are the lifeblood of any thriving organization. When implemented properly, they're the very mechanisms that keep your business in tune with reality, constantly adapting and evolving to the marketplace in real time.

Think of feedback loops as the nervous system of your business. Just as our bodies send signals about hunger, pain, or pleasure, your business needs systems that provide crucial information about what's working, what's not, and what needs to change.

I remember working with a startup several years back. They had a great product and ambitious goals. But they were operating in a vacuum, pushing forward with their ideas without really listening to what their market was telling them. It was like they were trying to navigate a ship without any instruments, relying solely on their gut instincts.

We implemented two types of feedback loops that completely transformed their approach:

1. **Reinforcing Loop:** We set up a referral program where satisfied customers could easily share the product with others. Each share led to more users, which led to more shares, creating a snowball effect that supercharged their growth.

2. **Balancing Loop:** We created a dynamic pricing model that adjusted based on the customer's usage. As demand increased, prices would slightly increase, ensuring they could maintain quality service and continue to provide a high level of support when needed without overloading their team's capacity.

Within six months, their customer base had doubled, and they were able to scale their infrastructure smoothly without any major outages or customer complaints.

Now, I'm not saying you need to copy this exact approach. Every business is unique, but the objective is to identify the specific areas in your business that could benefit from these feedback mechanisms. To truly benefit from this strategy, you only need one or two per department.

For instance, a retail business might implement a reinforcing loop through a customer loyalty program, while using inventory tracking as a balancing loop. A service-based company could use client satisfaction surveys as a reinforcing loop and employee work-load monitoring as a balancing loop.

Maybe it's regular check-ins with your team to pulse-check your processes. Or perhaps it's reviewing customer behavior data to understand how your product is being used in the wild. There's certainly no shortage of options, but regardless of what you decide to implement, the goal is to create multiple touchpoints that give you a 360-degree view of the status of your clients and your internal systems.

Side note: I've written a book titled *"The Exceptional Experience: Building a Business Your Customers Will Love,"* where we go deep into all aspects of monitoring the client journey and the full range of metrics needed to deliver a truly world-class experience. It explores several types of feedback loops and how they can be integrated into your fulfillment strategy. If you haven't yet gotten copies for yourself and your team, I highly recommend that you do so, as this book that you're reading here is designed to complement and expand on everything we cover in the *Exceptional Experience*. You can grab copies of it using this link or by scanning the QR Code:https://bit.ly/TheExceptionalExperienceBook

Here's a key principle to remember—creating these feedback loops only becomes valuable when this feedback isn't just collected but actually acted upon. I've seen too many businesses go through the motions of gathering feedback, only to let it gather dust in some forgotten spreadsheet (a total waste of time).

If you want a business that's responsive and adaptable, capable of self-correction and continuous improvement, installing feedback loops helps make that happen.

Take a good, hard look at your business. Where are your blind spots? What information are you missing? How can you create mechanisms that will keep you constantly informed and agile?

Answer these questions, and you'll be well on your way to mastering feedback loops.

Here's a challenge for you: Identify *one* area in your business right now where you could implement a feedback loop immediately. It could be as simple as setting up a weekly check-in with your team to gather insights from support tickets or creating a quick survey for your customers after each interaction. The key is to start small, but start now. The sooner you begin, the sooner you'll start reaping the benefits of a more responsive, adaptable business.

OVERCOMING COMMON SYSTEMS-THINKING CHALLENGES

As powerful as this holistic approach can be, it's definitely not without its hurdles. In my years of working with clients and their teams, I've noticed several recurring challenges that can trip up even the most skilled and well-intentioned.

Similar to *The Five Opposing Forces of Leadership* we covered in Chapter 1, I've also identified four stumbling blocks that can throw a wrench in your efforts when trying to build a more interconnected, big-picture mindset in your organization. Now, while the variables are obviously endless from business to business and industry to industry, these core challenges do seem to pop up more often than not.

So, to be clear, this isn't an exhaustive list. You'll have to customize this specific to your role and business. But these obstacles represent the majority of roadblocks I've encountered when helping clients implement a systems-thinking approach. The aim here is that by getting you familiar with these challenges and preparing for them in advance, you'll be better equipped to navigate the complexities of bringing this holistic perspective into your organization.

Let's break down each of these four stumbling blocks and tackle them head-on.

#1 Analysis Paralysis Trap

It's easy to get so caught up in mapping out every single connection and feedback loop in your system that you never actually take action. I once worked with a CEO who could diagram her company's systems with breathtaking detail, but she struggled to implement any meaningful changes because she was always waiting for more data, more analysis, and more certainty.

The antidote? Start small. Pick *one* area of your business where you can apply systems-thinking principles and run a pilot project. It doesn't have to be perfect. In fact, it probably won't be. But the insights you'll gain from actually putting systems-thinking into practice are invaluable.

But please, for the love of all things profitable, resist that visionary urge to tear everything down and start fresh. You know what I'm talking about—that 2 a.m. "eureka" moment where you're ready to completely revolutionize every process in your company. (*"Team, everything changes today!"*) Don't do it. Start small. Will the compound effect of incremental changes give you that dopamine hit of total revolution? Probably not. But it will give you something better: sustainable, predictable growth that actually sticks.

Remember: Your vision may be ahead of its time, but your execution needs to stay grounded in today's reality.

#2 Silver Bullet Syndrome

This is the mistaken belief that if you just find the right leverage point, you can solve all your problems with one elegant solution. While it's true that some leverage points are more powerful than others, real-world systems are rarely that simple.

I remember a brick-and-mortar retailer I worked with who thought they'd found their silver bullet in a new inventory management system. They poured significant amounts of time (and money) into implementing it, certain it would solve all their efficiency problems. But they neglected other crucial aspects of their business, like employee training and monitoring feedback from customer service. The result? A fancy new system that nobody knew how to use effectively, which frustrated customers who couldn't find what they needed.

The lesson is clear: while it's important to identify high-impact leverage points, don't neglect the basics. Nine times out of ten, simplifying and improving what you're already doing is more impactful than adding something new or sophisticated to the equation.

#3 Silo Mentality

Perhaps the most insidious challenge in systems thinking is what I call "Silo Mentality." This is when different departments or teams within an organization operate in isolation, failing to consider how their actions impact the broader system. Obviously, the larger the business, the more likely this is to occur.

Breaking down these silos requires a conscious effort to foster cross-functional collaboration. It might mean restructuring your teams, changing your meeting formats, or even redesigning your physical (or virtual) workspace to encourage more interaction. But the payoff—a more cohesive, responsive organization—is well worth the effort.

#4 Short-Term Thinking

In today's fast-paced market, there's immense pressure to deliver quick results. But systems often have delayed feedback; the consequences of your actions might not be apparent for several days, weeks, or even months.

Overcoming short-term thinking requires a shift in perspective. It means setting longer-term goals and metrics alongside your short-term targets. It means educating stakeholders about the importance of sustainable growth over quick wins. And it often means having the courage to make decisions that might not pay off immediately, but will set your organization up for long-term success.

ADOPTING THE SYSTEMS-THINKING MINDSET

Embracing the concepts we've covered in this chapter requires a fundamental shift in how we perceive and interact with the world around us. Systems-thinking allows you to view your business through a new lens, revealing the intricate web of relationships that shape your organization and its environment.

Keep in mind as you begin to adopt the principles and strategies we discuss in the coming chapters that "perfection" is not the end goal—*progress* is. Each step toward more systematic thinking propels your organization toward greater effectiveness, sustainability, and impact. The rewards are substantial and worth the effort: a more resilient, adaptive, and successful business.

QUESTIONS TO CONSIDER

1. Looking at your current biggest business challenge through the Power Grid Framework™, which zone (Vision & Purpose, Systems & Structure, Execution & Operations, or Growth & Evolution) needs immediate attention? Why?

2. Where in your business are you confusing complexity with sophistication? What systems could be simplified without sacrificing effectiveness?

3. Think about your organization's feedback loops. Which areas of your business are operating in a vacuum without proper feedback mechanisms? What specific metrics could you implement to change this?

4. Review your last three major business decisions. Were they reactive responses to immediate pressures or strategic moves aligned with your long-term vision? How could you shift this balance?

5. Which of your current systems actually amplifies your vision versus simply maintaining the status quo? How could you transform maintenance-focused systems into growth catalysts?

In the pages ahead, we're going to tackle the stuff that keeps visionary leaders up at night. You know, the *real* challenges that nobody talks about at networking events. We'll look at how to stay focused when your phone's pinging away with notifications nonstop, your team needs answers, and that brilliant idea you had at 3 a.m. is trying to escape. (Sound familiar?)

Then we'll dig into building business systems that actually work. Not the kind that look pretty in a presentation doc, but the kind that turn those big, audacious dreams of yours into "Wow, we actually did it" reality.

THREE
TRANSFORMING BIG IDEAS INTO TANGIBLE RESULTS
TOPIC: MAKING YOUR VISION REAL

"The best way to predict the future is to create it."
—Peter Drucker, *Management: Tasks, Responsibilities, Practices*

MAKING YOUR VISION REAL

I'm going to start this chapter with a truth that might ruffle some feathers, but it needs to be said: Having a great idea is the easy part. There, I said it. Don't get me wrong—those flashes of inspiration, those moments when you see a future no one else can, they're invaluable. But they're just the beginning.

The real challenge—*and the real opportunity*—lies in translating those big ideas into strategic plans your team can actually execute, taking that vivid picture in your mind and turning it into a blueprint that others can actually follow.

TRANSLATING BIG IDEAS INTO STRATEGIC PLANS

I remember a few years ago sitting across from Jacob, a long-time client and friend, in a bustling Southern California coffee shop. The music coming through the speakers in the background and the energy of everyone around us was upbeat, but Jacob looked deflated. He'd just come from another frustrating meeting with his team. Jacob had this brilliant idea for a revolutionary supply chain management system. His vision was clear and compelling; he could see how it would transform entire industries. But when it came to actually building it, he kept running into walls. His team was confused, investors were getting antsy, and he was at his wit's end.

"I don't get it, Mike," he said, running his hands through his hair. "I can see it so clearly. Why can't they?"

I've known Jacob for years. He's one of those people who can spot patterns and opportunities that others miss and then later, once he's come up with the solution, people say, "Why didn't I think of that?!" But like many visionaries, he struggled with the translation—turning that crystal-clear image in his mind into something others could see and act on.

We spent the next couple of hours dissecting his approach. It became clear that Jacob was trying to download his entire vision directly into his team's brains. As I sat there listening, I could see how excited he was, but even I was starting to feel lightheaded with the volume of detail and industry-specific vernacular he was using to describe the project. He was so close to the idea, so intimately familiar with every nuance, that he couldn't understand why others couldn't see it as clearly as he did. Maybe you've felt this way before?

An important side note for all you experts out there: When communicating your ideas to others, it's easy to forget what it's like to not know what you know. When we are passionate about a topic and spend every waking hour immersed in our world, we have to be mindful to not assume that what seems entirely basic and obvious to us is the same for others.

In fact, this issue truly is one of the primary catalysts that drive many teams to fail. So much so that I've dedicated an entire section on this very topic, which we'll cover later in Chapter 7: Engineering Excellence.

Now, back to our story: After leaving the coffee shop and over the next few weeks, we worked on a new approach. Instead of trying to convey the entire vision at once, we started with the "why." Jacob crafted a compelling narrative about the problem his system would solve and how it would change the industry. Not just a mission statement but a story that people could connect with emotionally.

Next, we broke down his grand vision into smaller, more manageable pieces. Instead of trying to revolutionize the entire supply chain at once, we identified key components that could be tackled individually. This not only made the project less overwhelming for the team, but it also allowed for early wins that boosted his team's morale and proved the concept to investors.

One of the most crucial steps was developing a shared vocabulary for discussing the project. This might seem like a small detail, but the impact was huge. When everyone started using the same terms, misunderstandings decreased dramatically, and the team aligned more quickly.

The breakthrough moment came when we created a visual roadmap. Jacob and I spent a full day mapping out how each piece of the project fit into the larger whole. It wasn't just a timeline or a set of milestones; it was a visual representation of his vision, showing how each component was interconnected and contributed to the end goal.

When Jacob presented this to his team, you could almost see the light bulbs popping on above their heads. Suddenly, they weren't just working on isolated tasks; they could see how their individual efforts were crucial to bringing this big idea to life.

The transformation was remarkable. Within a couple of months, Jacob's team had a working prototype that captured the essence of his original vision. More importantly, the entire team was aligned and energized. Now, they weren't just following orders; they were co-creators.

But here's the interesting part, and it's something I've seen time and time again. The final product *was not* exactly what Jacob had initially envisioned. ***It was better***. By involving his team in the process of translating his big idea into a strategic plan, the vision itself evolved. The team's diverse perspectives and expertise added layers and nuances that Jacob hadn't initially considered.

"The real power of effectively translating your big ideas isn't just getting others to see your vision, it's allowing that vision to grow and improve through collaboration."

The key is to maintain a balance between the big picture and the details. As the visionary leader, your job is to keep that overarching vision alive and vibrant, while also diving into the trenches with your team to figure out the "how."

This brings us to an essential skill for any visionary leader: the ability to "zoom in and out." You need to be able to shift fluidly from the 30,000-foot view of your vision to the ground-level details of execution and back again.

It's this mental flexibility that allows you to keep the big picture in mind while working on and communicating through the nitty-gritty details. Learning how to do this effectively requires practice. Like going to the gym, you'll need to flex that muscle regularly over time to get good at it. Without question, this skill is nonnegotiable for anyone who desires to translate their vision from the ether of thought into physical form. Commit to mastering this; it's imperative.

CRAFTING AGILE ROADMAPS

Now let's dive into the process of creating roadmaps that can survive the unpredictability of the real world and actually lead you somewhere. Because let's face it, we've all seen those beautiful, color-coded project plans that end up being more decorative than functional.

I remember working with Alex, a really talented marketing consultant who had built a thriving personal brand. He had a vision to scale his business, transforming his one-on-one client work into an online learning platform for aspiring marketers. His idea was solid, his content was top-notch, and he had a growing audience eager for more.

Three months into the project, though, Alex found himself struggling to make progress. He was creating content, building the platform, trying to market it... but it felt like he was just throwing spaghetti at the wall and hoping something would stick. Great vision and loads of expertise, but no structured path to bring it all together.

This is where dreams can quickly fade into unrealized "nice ideas" unless you give them a track to run on. It's not enough to see the promised land; you need to chart the course to get there. It was time to introduce Alex to systems-thinking.

First, we got crystal clear on the destination. Sure, everyone on the team knew they were building an online learning platform, but what did success actually look like? To achieve this, we needed a defined, concrete, measurable outcome. "Measurable" being the key word here. You must be able to clearly and specifically identify when the objective has been achieved.

We turned a loose, hard-to-quantify goal like "become the leading online education platform in our industry" into a clearly measurable milestone of success like "achieve a 95% course completion rate while maintaining an average NPS score of 70 or higher across 500 active students within the next 18 months." This shift from abstract ambition to concrete metrics gave the entire team a crystal-clear target to aim for.

Next, we worked backward from that end goal, identifying the major milestones along the way. This is crucial—too often, teams try to plan from where they are now, which can lead to a kind of aimless "progress" that doesn't actually bring you closer to your goal.

Then we created repeatable processes for content creation, platform development, and marketing efforts. This created a framework that allowed Alex and his team to work efficiently and consistently.

But there's something crucial that many roadmaps miss: they assume a linear path. In the real world, especially when you're doing something innovative, the path is rarely straight. So we built in flexibility. For each major milestone, we identified potential obstacles and alternative routes.

We also established clear markers for success at each stage (as in "how will we know if this step is achieved or not? How will we measure it?). This ensured that each step actually moved us closer to the ultimate goal. If a particular approach wasn't yielding results, we had predetermined points where we'd reevaluate and pivot if necessary.

An important concept to remember at this stage is SIMPLIC-ITY. Stay high level during the first couple of iterations. There almost certainly will be more required than what is on the roadmap, but during the first iterations, develop mile markers, essentially signposts that lead the way to a repeatable, reliable process. All the minutiae can be fleshed out later.

There's no shortage of methodologies and tools that can be applied here, but honestly, my favorite way is to just map it out on a single slide or piece of paper. Brevity begets clarity. As Winston Churchill famously observed, "If you want me to speak for two minutes, I'll need two weeks to prepare. If you want me to speak for two hours, I'm ready now." When ideas are well-formed and purposeful, there's no need for excessive explanation. I tell clients all the time that if they can't articulate their process on a single piece of paper, they won't understand it well enough.

Whether you go pen to paper or use digital drawing tools, the end result should be the same; a clear roadmap that illustrates the key decision points and optional pivots and timelines involved in reaching the measurable end result. For Alex, we started with a high-level overview so his entire team could understand the objectives as well as when and how benchmark milestones were to be calculated.

Before we move on, I want to emphasize one more crucial point about crafting effective roadmaps: communication. Your roadmap isn't just for you; it's a tool to align your entire team and even your stakeholders. Regular check-ins to review progress, celebrate wins, and address challenges are vital. In many cases, this will mean making changes to it along the way. It's much more an evolutionary, iterative process than a one-and-done task, which is exactly what we'll address next.

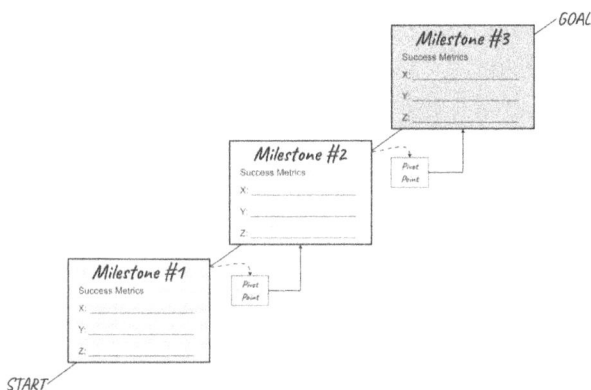

THE FINE LINE BETWEEN PERSISTENCE AND STUBBORNNESS

Turning your big ideas into reality requires more than having a great plan because nothing is static. You need to also consistently be measuring progress and be willing to adjust course when needed. This is where many visionaries stumble. We get so focused on the end goal that we forget to check if we're still on the right path. If you're anything like me, once I set my eyes on a goal... watch out; I put the blinders on and go for it!

Over the years, I've had to learn to take the time to stop and look up long enough to consider alternative ideas before steamrolling ahead again. Market demands change quickly—being fluid and willing to adapt while still staying on course is a superpower worth pursuing. We never want to jump from idea to idea, avoiding resistance at all costs, but there's also a stark difference between being persistent and just being stupid.

I've worked with more than a few clients over the years where fear would take over when challenges arose that required them to change their approach. Being emotionally prepared to let go of previous iterations is a huge milestone in every visionary's journey.

I'll share one of these client's stories as it's a great example of this.

At the time, Rachel had a thriving business. Her vision was to expand her company internationally, tapping into markets across Europe and Asia. She had a solid plan, a great team, and the capital to make it happen. A few months into the expansion, she called me in a state of overwhelm.

"Mike," she said, her voice a mix of frustration and confusion, "we're hitting all our financial targets, but something feels off. We're expanding, but it's like we're losing our identity in the process."

When I dug into the details with Rachel and her team, I realized they had fallen into a common trap. They were measuring the right things—sales figures, market penetration, and customer acquisition costs—but they weren't measuring the right way, at least not from a holistic perspective.

Here's what I mean by that. Yes, they were hitting their numerical targets, but they weren't tracking how this rapid expansion was affecting their brand identity, their company culture, or their long-term sustainability. They were winning the battle but potentially losing the war.

This is where measuring progress can become a bit more challenging. For true long-term, sustainable success, we have to track numbers in the right context. *Growth just for the sake of expansion is a dangerous game, and success, especially at speed, can be just as damaging as stagnation.* Like when growing up as a kid and having a growth spurt, you can grow right out of your clothes. Our plans and systems are the same way. Here's how we turned things around for Rachel:

First, we started looking for a more holistic measurement. We expanded their metrics beyond just the typical financial indicators. We started tracking things like brand sentiment in new markets, employee satisfaction during the expansion, and the adaptability of their systems to new cultural contexts.

Next, we defined her new leading indicators. Instead of just looking at lagging indicators (like sales), we identified leading indicators that could predict future success or challenges. For example, we tracked the engagement levels of new customers, not just the number of new customers.

With new data points in place, we then looked for ways to collect qualitative feedback. We implemented regular surveys and feedback sessions with customers and employees in new markets. This qualitative data provided context and depth to our quantitative metrics.

Lastly, alignment checks. We created a system to regularly check if their actions in new markets were aligned with their core values and long-term vision. This helped ensure they weren't sacrificing their identity for short-term gains. This is where having a clearly defined mission statement and company culture doc for the organization really comes in handy. You want that in place BEFORE you hit scale mode. Once you're moving at full speed, these assets can become harder to define.

Like a lighthouse on a dark, stormy night, you need a directional reference point for decision-making when the surrounding environment is changing (and that lighthouse has to be built BEFORE the storm arrives).

Rachel's story drives home an important point: tracking numbers alone doesn't tell you if you're making real progress. You've got to keep an eye on the bigger picture. Are you still moving toward your vision, or are you just climbing a ladder that's leaning against the wrong wall?

Here's where what I call your "North Star Metric" comes in. It's the one number that tells you whether you're actually delivering on your core promise as a business. Social media companies look at daily active users. SaaS companies often focus on customer lifetime value. The specific metric doesn't matter as much as making sure it genuinely aligns with what you're trying to achieve.

As a quick aside on this concept: when I'm working with startup entrepreneurs who are in the earliest stages of bringing their products/services to market, in almost all cases, their North Star Metric is (or should be) "number of sales calls per day." By reviewing that single metric, I can measure with quite a bit of accuracy how their monthly revenue will play out. This is because the number of daily calls being held directly indicates exposure to their market. More calls equals more opportunities for sales to take place. Period.

Additionally, increased market exposure through these calls provides invaluable real-world feedback about your value proposition - each conversation is a chance to gauge how well your offering resonates with your total addressable market and reveals whether adjustments are needed for better message-market fit. There is no more important KPI than that.

There will always be a million things to do and "urgent matters" to attend to, but when you boil things down, if sales and revenue are the goal, the number of conversations being held with prospects that can say yes or no to your offer is what you need to optimize. As businesses grow, needs and focus evolve. But in the beginning, sales cures all, as it is the lifeblood of any business. When you are just getting started, the emphasis needs to be on keeping things simple and identifying a single KPI that does exactly that to measure daily progress.

"Never confuse activity for productivity;
they're not the same thing."

However, a lone star, no matter how luminous, does not constitute a galaxy. Your North Star Metric demands a carefully curated ecosystem of supporting metrics. These additional measures provide depth and context to your progress.

Once you define what data you are going to monitor, the real benefits come from its effective utilization. This is where establishing a regular cadence of review becomes crucial. Every business is unique, but a well-structured weekly team meeting consisting of the department leads is, in almost all cases, a great way to go. Perhaps a weekly operational check-in, coupled with a monthly tactical deep dive and rounded out by quarterly strategic sessions. Regardless of what you decide to track, consistency is key here.

Although there is certainly no shortage of fancy dashboards and platforms for tracking metrics, I've found that unless you have an entire department to utilize the scope of features, many of them are like bringing a bazooka to a knife fight. Is it actually better, or just bigger? Naturally, use common sense when selecting tools, but, in many cases, a basic spreadsheet can do the trick just fine for producing a simple and still potently effective dashboard for monitoring each department's KPIs. These should consist of three but no more than five leading indicators that the department lead can clearly measure and report on.

The benefit of a weekly cadence is that it's frequent enough to identify anomalies early for making course corrections. Whereas, if the team is only reviewing metrics every four weeks, a lot could go wrong that could have been optimized if identified sooner. Inversely, a daily cadence is a bit of an overkill in most instances unless it's department or project-specific, where inter-team communications are essential for netting the desired results.

Regardless of how you decide to display these metrics, the power of well-designed dashboards cannot be overstated. They transform raw numbers into instant insights, making complex data both accessible and actionable at a glance. When your entire team can easily grasp the numbers, you foster a shared language for discussing progress and tackling challenges head-on. Think of it as a GPS for your business journey, not only pinpointing your current position but also helping you navigate shifting conditions to chart the optimal course to your destination.

To hammer home these concepts that we've covered so far, let's consider a real-world example of a company that masterfully balanced vision with adaptability: Netflix.

Netflix started with a clear vision: delivering entertainment directly to consumers' homes. Initially, this manifested as a DVD-by-mail service. But as technology evolved and consumer behaviors shifted, they didn't cling rigidly to their original model. Instead, they pivoted to streaming media, fundamentally transforming their business while keeping their core vision intact. The vision didn't change (delivering entertainment directly to consumers' homes) but the medium, the vehicle used, evolved with technology.

This flexibility, guided by careful measurement and analysis of market trends, allowed Netflix to not just survive but exponentially grow in a rapidly changing landscape. They kept their eyes fixed on their North Star—convenient, personalized entertainment—while radically altering their method of delivery.

The Netflix story illustrates a crucial point for all visionary leaders:

"Your vision is not a destination; it's a compass.
Let it guide you, but be prepared to forge new paths."

Before we move into the next chapters, I challenge you to take a hard look at how you're currently measuring progress in your organization. Are you simply tracking numbers, or are you telling the story of your journey? Are you flexible enough to adjust your course when needed, or are you rigidly sticking to your initial plan?

Keep in mind: the goal isn't to hit every target perfectly every time. It's to learn, adapt, and continually move closer to your ultimate vision. Embrace the journey with all its twists and turns. That's where the real growth happens.

Let's tackle something that trips up even the best leaders: staying focused when everything around you is chaos. In Chapter 4, we're going to dig into exactly how to beat overwhelm and keep your eye on what matters most.

QUESTIONS TO CONSIDER

As you prepare to move forward, take some time to reflect on the following:

1. Looking at your most ambitious current project, where might you be "downloading your entire vision" onto your team like Jacob initially did? What specific communication adjustments could you make to bridge this gap?

2. What's your current North Star Metric? More importantly, what supporting metrics make up its "constellation" to provide fuller context of your progress?

3. When was the last time you evolved your vision based on team input? If you haven't, what barriers might be preventing this collaborative evolution?

4. How effectively are you balancing the "zoom in and zoom out" capability discussed in the chapter? Where do you tend to get stuck—in the details or in the big picture?

5. Thinking about your current roadmap, is it truly agile or just a rigid plan? What specific pivot points could you build in to make it more adaptable?

FOUR
CONQUERING OVERWHELM AND MASTERING FOCUS

TOPIC: MASTERING FOCUS IN A WORLD OF DISTRACTION

"If you want to make a difference in the world,
you must focus your time and energy
on the things that truly matter."
—Jim Collins

MASTERING FOCUS IN A WORLD OF DISTRACTIONS

Imagine you're juggling chainsaws while riding a unicycle on a tightrope. Sounds crazy, right? Well, for many entrepreneurs, this circus act isn't that far off from their daily reality. The constant barrage of emails, meetings, decisions, and fires to put out can leave even the most seasoned visionary feeling like they're drowning in tasks (been there, done that!).

Here's a truth that might sting a bit: that overwhelm isn't just uncomfortable—it's downright dangerous. It's the silent assassin of great ideas, the thief of innovation, and the quicksand that can trap even the most brilliant minds in a cycle of reactivity.

"Wow Mike, aren't you being a bit dramatic there?" Possibly, but as visionaries, our most valuable asset isn't our time or even our ideas —it's our mental bandwidth. Our ability to think deeply, to see connections others miss, and to imagine bold new futures is what sets us apart. But when we're constantly firefighting, when our days are fragmented into a thousand tiny tasks, that unique ability gets compromised.

I remember sitting across from Shanelle, a seasoned and highly sought-after life coach. Her eyes, usually sparkling with innovation, now dimmed under the weight of a thousand small tasks. "Mike," she said, her voice a mix of frustration and exhaustion, "I know where I want to take this company. I can see it so clearly. But I'm so bogged down in the day-to-day that I can't even find time to think about the big picture, let alone work toward it."

Shanelle's situation isn't unique. It's a pattern I see play out with visionary leaders all the time. We start with grand dreams and bold visions, but before we know it, we're spending our days answering emails, sitting in pointless meetings, and putting out fires that our teams should be handling. The result? Our visions fade away into the shadows while we exhaust ourselves on tasks that don't move the needle.

But it doesn't have to be this way. In fact, if you want to make a real impact, *it can't be this way!*

> *"The world doesn't need more busy entrepreneurs;*
> *it needs visionary leaders who can think big, see far,*
> *and guide their teams toward audacious goals."*

In this chapter, we're going to tackle this challenge head-on. We'll explore strategies for conquering overwhelm, techniques for reclaiming your mental bandwidth, and systems for staying focused on what truly matters. We'll look at one of the fastest ways to boost results with a method called Strategic Elimination, learning how to ruthlessly prioritize and delegate so that your time and energy are reserved for the tasks that only you can do.

And in case you're wondering, we're going to go way beyond the typical "productivity hacks" or time management tips (no shortage of those out there already.) No, what we're after is a fundamental shift in how you approach your role as a visionary leader. We're going to rewire your thinking, helping you create systems that free up your mind to do what it does best: *envision the future and chart the course to get there.*

Let's get after it.

UNDERSTANDING THE ENEMY

Before you can ever have a chance at conquering overwhelm, you need to understand what you're up against. Because overwhelm is more than just a feeling—it's a complex psychological and physiological state that can significantly impair your ability to think and act strategically.

When you're overwhelmed, your brain shifts into survival mode. The prefrontal cortex—the part responsible for complex thought, planning, and decision-making—essentially goes offline. Instead, you're driven by your amygdala, the primitive part governing your fight-or-flight response. Great for a caveman facing a saber-toothed tiger, but not so helpful for a CEO trying to lead a company into the future.

Consider Tom, an experienced engineer turned startup founder. He had developed some groundbreaking clean energy technology, but as his company grew, he found himself increasingly bogged down in operational details. When I first met him, he was working 80-hour weeks, constantly putting out fires and micromanaging every aspect of the business.

"I feel like I'm always reacting," Tom confessed during one of our sessions. "I know I should be thinking about our long-term strategy, but I can barely keep my head above water with all the day-to-day stuff." (By this time, you might be seeing a theme with these stories.)

Tom's situation illustrates classic overwhelm. He was so caught up in the urgent that he had no space for the important. His vision—the very thing that made his company unique and valuable—was getting lost in a sea of emails, meetings, and crisis management.

Let's get something straight—overwhelm isn't just about having too many tasks. It's about spending your time and energy on the wrong things because you've lost sight of what being a visionary leader really means.

Think about your last week. How many "urgent" tasks consumed your day? Now ask yourself if they were really important, or did they just feel important because they were screaming the loudest? Most visionaries I work with are drowning in tasks they never should have taken on in the first place, all because they've bought into someone else's definition of what "matters most."

As visionaries, our value doesn't come from doing more. It comes from thinking differently, from seeing possibilities others miss, and from guiding our teams toward those possibilities. When you allow yourself to get sucked into the vortex of day-to-day operations, you're not just going to feel more stressed—you're actively undermining your most valuable contribution.

This is where systems thinking becomes crucial, and why it's not something that you should be entirely outsourcing to your operations team.

> *"Instead of trying to manage overwhelm, we need to design systems that prevent it from occurring in the first place."*

Ask yourself: What if, instead of starting each day reacting to whatever lands in your inbox, you began with an hour of uninterrupted strategic thinking? What if you had systems in place that handled 80% of the operational issues without your involvement, freeing you to focus on the big picture?

This isn't just a nice idea—it's an imperative. Your mind is your most valuable asset. It's time you start treating it that way. So let's look at how to actually do that.

STRATEGIC ELIMINATION

The biggest threat to your vision isn't your competition or market conditions. It's all the "good" things you're still hanging onto that are secretly holding you back.

Now that you understand the enemy you're up against, it's time to arm yourself with one of the most powerful weapons in a visionary's arsenal: strategic elimination. This practice will allow you to ruthlessly focus on what truly matters while eliminating everything else.

Early in my career, I prided myself on being a do-it-all entrepreneur. First one in, last one out, juggling a million tasks and wearing every hat in the company. I thought this made me a great leader. In reality, I was bottlenecking my company's growth and stifling my ability to think strategically. I wore my 17-hour work days like a badge of honor. Man, was I missing the point.

It wasn't until I found myself on the brink of burnout that I realized something had to change. I needed to shift from being the company's Swiss Army knife to its North Star.

Not a unique or grand concept I know, but here's where most leaders get it wrong: They think strategic elimination is about cutting out the "bad" stuff. The redundant meetings, the time-wasting activities, and the obvious distractions. That's kindergarten-level thinking. The real power move? Having the courage to eliminate things that are actually working "pretty well."

The hardest pill to swallow is that some of what you need to eliminate isn't broken, it just belongs to an older version of you. Like a snake that can't grow without shedding its skin, you can't expand into your next level while holding onto everything that got you here.

I see this play out with clients all the time. They know they need to evolve, but they resist letting go because what they're doing still "works." But here's the thing: what works is often the enemy of what could be extraordinary.

This isn't only about time management or delegation. It's about having the courage to create space for your next evolution, even when that space feels uncomfortable. Even when that voice in your head (let's call it what it is—ego masquerading as wisdom) tells you nobody can do it as well as you can.

Every task you take on and every responsibility you shoulder comes with an opportunity cost.

> *"When you say yes to something, you're inevitably saying no to something else."*

The key is to get intentional about what you're saying yes and no to. This means taking a hard look at how you're spending your time and asking yourself some tough questions:

- *Is this task something only I can do?*
- *Does this directly contribute to our long-term vision and strategy?*
- *Am I the best person in the organization to handle this?*
- *If I don't do this, what higher-value activities could I focus on instead?*

For most tasks, you'll find the answer to these questions is "no." And that's okay. In fact, it's great news, because it means you've just identified something you can eliminate, delegate, or systematize.

Side note: We're going to be addressing delegating to team members and empowering others later in Chapter 7: *Engineering Excellence.* For now, the objective is managing *personal* overwhelm and focus.

Strategic elimination is a mindset, a continuous practice of questioning and refining how you spend your time and mental energy. It requires discipline and, sometimes, hard choices. You might have to say no to good opportunities to make room for great ones. You might have to let go of tasks you enjoy but that don't align with your role as a visionary leader.

Here's a powerful exercise I often use with clients: For one week, meticulously track how you spend every hour of your workday. But don't just track the time, note how each activity makes you *feel*. Pay attention to where you get energized versus drained, where you feel irreplaceable versus where you're just hanging on out of habit. At the end of the week, categorize each activity into one of three buckets:

1. **Visionary Work:** Strategic thinking, long-term planning, big-picture decision-making
2. **Necessary Evil:** Tasks that you must do that don't directly contribute to the vision
3. **Delegate or Eliminate:** Everything else

Aim to spend at least 70% of your time on Visionary Work, no more than 20% on Necessary Evil, and less than 10% on tasks that could be delegated or eliminated.

HARNESSING THE POWER OF AUTOMATION

Let's talk about something I see all the time with clients—that love/hate relationship with automation. On one hand, we all know we need it. The idea of systems running smoothly in the background while we focus on bigger things? Sounds amazing, right?

But here's the reality I've seen play out over and over. Leaders get sold on some fancy new tech solution, drop a ton of money (and time) on implementation, and six months later, they're right back to doing things the old way.

The problem isn't the technology; it's our approach to it. I've learned there's a much better way to think about automation.

Let's start by acknowledging a fundamental truth: automation isn't really about the "tech" at all. It's about freeing up your brain to focus on what you do best.

When most people hear "automation," they think of complicated software and expensive systems. But that's missing the point completely. The true objective is to create space in your calendar and in your head for the big-picture stuff that only you can handle.

Sometimes, this can be achieved by a truly automated system and software, and other times, it simply requires creating a well-defined SOP (standard operating procedure), essentially a checklist-like process for completing a task the same way each time.

So, as we move forward, just know that "automation" can also be viewed as "systemization." Either way, the outcome should be the same—exceptional outcomes with high levels of efficiency.

Try this: Take a hard look at your day. What tasks keep pulling you away from strategic thinking? Where do you or your team keep making the same mistakes? What decisions are you making over and over that could be handled by a simple system?

I had a client recently who was spending hours every week personally approving basic expense reports. We set up a simple approval framework over the course of about 60 minutes and—boom—it instantly freed up three hours every week for strategic planning.

These are your automation opportunities. And trust me, they're hiding in plain sight...

But here's the crucial part: you don't need to be a tech guru to take advantage of them. Your role as a visionary leader is not to implement the automation yourself, but to identify where it can have the most significant impact on freeing up mental bandwidth for visionary work.

Another visionary I worked with was drowning in the minutiae of project management, constantly chasing updates and realigning timelines. By implementing a straightforward project management tool with automated reminders and status updates, he transformed his role from project micromanager to strategic overseer.

These solutions didn't require a computer science degree or a massive IT overhaul. They simply required identifying the right pain points and applying targeted solutions.

But a word of caution to the enthusiasts among us: "more" is not always better. I've watched too many visionary leaders go down the rabbit hole of "automation addiction," signing up for every new tool and platform in a quest for the perfect system. This approach often leads to a complex web of underutilized tools, cobbled together like Frankenstein, that creates more confusion than clarity.

The key is to start small, focus on impact, and scale gradually. Choose a few key areas where automation can free up significant mental bandwidth. Implement solutions thoughtfully, always keeping your end goal in mind—creating more space for visionary thinking.

Here's the truth I learned the hard way... the best automation usually isn't some fancy tech solution.

"Sometimes, the best "automation" is simply a well-designed checklist or a clear decision-making framework that allows your team to operate autonomously."

When exploring automation solutions, **keep your focus on outcomes, not features**. Don't get seduced by flashy technology. Instead, ask yourself, "Will this truly free up mental space for visionary work?" Involve your team in the process; they often have the best insights into what processes are ripe for automation. Start with low-hanging fruit: simple automations that can have a big impact. Regularly reassess your strategies as your organization evolves. And remember, not everything should be automated. Some aspects of your business, especially those involving complex human interactions, may never be fully automated, and that's okay.

Think about some of the best customer experiences you've ever had. I bet they weren't automated, were they? They were probably moments where someone went above and beyond, showed real empathy, or solved a problem in a creative way.

The goal isn't to automate everything. It's to automate the right things so you and your team have the mental bandwidth to be truly present where it matters most.

By approaching automation with this mindset, you transform it from a technical challenge into a powerful tool for cultural transformation. You're sending a clear message: in this organization, we value innovative thinking over routine tasks. We don't use automation to replace human effort; we use automation to elevate it.

Here are two questions I want you to really sit with for a minute and consider:

1. What's the one thing you keep doing over and over that's stealing time from your most important work?
2. What aspects of your business should remain deliberately unautomated to preserve the human touch?

By implementing targeted automation strategies, you're not just increasing efficiency, you're freeing your mind, and the minds of your team, to focus on what truly matters.

EMBRACING YOUR ROLE AS A VISIONARY LEADER

Think back to where we started with the image of a leader juggling chainsaws while riding a unicycle. That's not leadership; it's survival. Authentic visionary leadership is about standing on solid ground, surveying the horizon, and charting a course that others can follow.

Remember Tom, the overwhelmed clean energy entrepreneur that I introduced at the beginning of this chapter? When I last spoke with him, he painted a very different picture of his daily life. "I used to feel like I was drowning in details," he said. "Now, I feel like I'm standing on a mountaintop, able to see for miles in every direction. I'm not just reacting anymore; I'm anticipating, planning, and dreaming. And the best part is that my team is thriving. They're solving problems I didn't even know existed, coming up with ideas I never would have thought of. It's like we've unlocked a whole new level of potential."

Tom's transformation didn't happen overnight, and it wasn't always easy. There were moments of doubt, times when he was tempted to fall back into old habits of micromanagement. But by consistently applying the principles we've discussed, he created a sustainable shift in how he led his organization.

As you apply these principles, remember that this will be an ongoing process. It requires constant vigilance, regular reassessment, and a willingness to adapt as your organization grows and evolves. But the rewards—for you, your team, and your entire organization—are immeasurable.

Imagine waking up each morning with a clear mind, excited about the big ideas you'll explore that day. Picture your team operating like a well-oiled machine, each member confidently handling their responsibilities and collaboratively solving problems without needing your direct involvement. Envision yourself having the time and mental space to spot emerging trends, forge strategic partnerships, and dream up innovative solutions to your industry's biggest challenges.

This is not a fantasy. It's the reality that awaits when you fully embrace your role as a visionary leader and create the systems to support it.

QUESTIONS TO CONSIDER

1. Using the three buckets exercise (Visionary Work, Necessary Evil, Delegate/Eliminate), audit your last week. What percentage of time did you spend on each? What one change would create the biggest shift toward the 70/20/10 ideal ratio?

2. Where in your business are you confusing "being busy" with "being effective"? Which "good" activities might you need to eliminate to make room for "great" ones?

3. Looking at your current automation systems, are they truly freeing up mental bandwidth or just adding another layer of complexity? What's one process you could simplify rather than automate?

4. Think about your most draining recurring tasks. Which ones keep pulling you back into operational details when you should be thinking strategically? What specific systems could you create to handle these permanently?

5. Like Tom in the chapter, are you standing on the mountaintop or still in the valley of details? What's the biggest barrier keeping you from that higher perspective, and what's one concrete step you could take this week to change that?

FIVE
UNSTOPPABLE BUSINESS SYSTEMS

TOPIC: BUILDING THE ENGINE FOR GROWTH

*"The most powerful tool we have in our toolkit is
the ability to create systems that work for us."*
—Chris Ducker, *Rise of the Youpreneur*

BUILDING THE ENGINE FOR GROWTH

Let's address the elephant in the room. A majority of visionaries see "systems" as something beneath them, a task to be delegated to the operations team while they focus on "more important" strategic work. I get it. We're wired for the big picture, the bold ideas, the "wouldn't it be amazing if..." moments. Building and optimizing systems probably doesn't get your heart racing like a new market opportunity does.

But here's where most visionaries miss something crucial: Some of history's most revolutionary leaders weren't just dreamers of big ideas, they were also brilliant systems thinkers. They just approached it differently than most people would expect.

Take Walt Disney. Everyone knows him as the dreamer who imagined magical kingdoms and talking mice. But what made Disney truly extraordinary wasn't just his creativity, it was his ability to build systems that turned imagination into reality. While others saw systems as constraints, he saw them as amplifiers. Not many people know that he was directly involved in revolutionizing animation by creating the "Multiple Plane Camera System," allowing animators to create a sense of depth and realism by stacking different layers of artwork (backgrounds, midground, foreground) and moving them independently. But his real genius showed in how he approached theme park design.

He created what we now know as "Imagineering"—a systematic approach to turning creative ideas into physical experiences. Disney was obsessed with systems, measuring everything from guest flow patterns to optimal trash can placement (based on observing how long people would carry trash before dropping it). These weren't rigid bureaucratic procedures; they were dynamic frameworks that allowed creativity to scale.

Think of the systems we're going to build, like the backstage crew at a rock concert. You don't always see them, but without them, the show doesn't go on. Without good systems, you're not "creatively nimble," you're just chaotic. And chaos is the real creativity killer because it instantly corners us into reactive versus proactive mode.

In this chapter, we're going to completely reframe how you think about systems. Forget everything you've been taught about rigid procedures and mind-numbing processes. You're going to build dynamic, living systems that amplify your vision instead of constraining it—systems that adapt and evolve as fast as your ideas do.

Let's get real clear on this. I am not here to turn you into an operations manager. (Trust me, that's the last thing either of us wants.) I'm here to show you how to harness the hidden power that most visionaries miss because, as we've already discussed, the visionaries who win aren't just the ones with the biggest dreams. They're the ones who know how to build the engines that bring those dreams to life.

THE DNA OF UNSTOPPABLE SYSTEMS

Now that we've cleared the air about the kind of systems we're talking about, let's get into what exactly makes a system unstoppable. There are four essential elements that have to be in place for them to be both efficient and adaptable so that you don't risk getting painted into a corner by your own self-designed system that becomes antiquated by changes in the marketplace.

Think of these elements as the DNA of your business; they need to be woven into everything you do. (Hint: what we're about to cover is the source code for truly unstoppable businesses.)

THE 4 ESSENTIAL ELEMENTS OF UNSTOPPABLE SYSTEMS

1. Vision Alignment

Every system must directly serve your bigger purpose. This sounds obvious, but where most businesses get it wrong is that they create systems to manage *current problems* rather than drive future objectives. This results in a collection of processes that keep you busy but don't actually move you forward.

Here's how to get it right: Take your audacious vision and work backward. Every system should answer the question: "How does this get us closer to our ultimate goal?" If it doesn't have a clear answer, it's just organizational busy work.

2. Built-In Intelligence

We spoke to this already, but it's worth repeating. Your systems need to be learning organisms, not static procedures. Think of each system as having its own nervous system constantly gathering feedback and adapting. This means building in clear metrics and feedback loops that tell you what's working and what isn't.

The key is measuring what matters. Don't track data just because you can. Ask yourself: "What information would fundamentally change how we operate?" Those are your true KPIs.

3. Scalable Architecture

Engineer your systems like you're building software, not constructing a building. They should be modular, upgradeable, and designed for exponential growth from day one. Most businesses build systems that become their own bottlenecks - rigid structures that crack under pressure rather than flex and grow.

Here's the framework I use with clients:

- Build for 10x growth from day one.
- Create modular components that can be upgraded independently.
- Document only what's essential for replication.
- Automate what's repetitive.

Now stop for a second because I already know how you may be feeling as I wrote that last paragraph. As soon as you read the words "document," did your stomach turn? Did a sense of dread come over you like a wet blanket? Don't stress; you can simplify this process by screen recording things as you're doing them and then asking someone on your team, or even a contracted virtual assistant, to build out SOPs (standard operating procedures) that others on the team can refer to.

It's honestly not that hard, you just have to be intentional enough to get it done. And if you want even more of a reason for its importance, your business's library of documentation actually increases its enterprise value exponentially. Think about it: Would you pay for a multimillion-dollar piece of machinery without an operator's manual? No way of knowing how it works or what to look for if something breaks? Of course not.

Regardless of how you decide to do it, you really need to have anything that has to get done repeatedly and done well to have documentation on fulfilling that task. A side benefit of doing this is that while itemizing processes, you'll very quickly identify things that can be improved, or my personal favorite, removed altogether.

4. Human-Centric Design

This is a big one because, at the end of the day, it's not the flow-charts or the software that make your business run—it's the people. Your systems should bring out the best in your team, not turn them into robots.

This means building autonomy and decision-making power at every level. We already broached this topic earlier, creating clear communication channels so ideas can flow freely is paramount. And it means fostering a culture where people feel safe to experiment, fail, and learn.

We'll expand on this further in Chapter 7.

In recap, the best systems:

- Reduce cognitive load spent on routine tasks.
- Free up mental space for creative thinking.
- Empower decision-making at every level.
- Create clear paths for growth and innovation.

Think of these 4 Essential Elements as genetic adaptation; your systems should be able to evolve while maintaining their core functionality.

What most visionaries never realize is that well-designed systems actually increase creative freedom. They handle the routine, the predictable, and the manageable, freeing you and your team to focus on innovation and breakthrough thinking.

PUTTING SYSTEMS INTO ACTION

Now that we've covered the basics, let's get into the nitty-gritty of how to actually implement these unstoppable systems. Fair warning:

this isn't a one-size-fits-all blueprint. Every business is unique, and your systems should be too. But there are some universal principles that can ensure that no time is wasted in trial-and-error mode.

Let's start with what I call the Vision-First Framework. This is where most visionaries get excited because now we're building systems that pull us toward our vision rather than just managing the status quo. Here's how it works:

THE VISION FIRST FRAMEWORK

Start by flipping the traditional approach on its head. Instead of building systems around current problems, we architect them around future objectives.

1. Start with your most audacious goal (the one that makes most people raise their eyebrows): This goal needs to be specific, measurable, and time-bound. None of this "we want to be the best in the industry" fluff. I'm talking about "we want to capture 30% market share in the next 18 months" kind of objective.

2. Break it into major milestones: What absolutely must happen to reach that goal? Work backward. Ask yourself, "What specifically needs to happen for us to achieve this?"

3. Identify the critical paths: the nonnegotiable elements that enable success. A lot of flex can be built into a game plan, but there needs to be preestablished requirements. Things that are absolute and unchanging, these serve as anchors that will help all future decision-making.

4. Design systems that make those paths inevitable: When you break big goals down into subtasks and then assign

specific metrics to the steps to complete those tasks, there is almost nothing that you can't achieve.

I know examples always help, so let's look at how this plays out in the real world. Elon Musk and his teams at Tesla and SpaceX provide a masterclass in this kind of thinking. (And no, you don't need billions in funding to apply these principles; stay with me here.)

When everyone else in the automotive and aerospace industries was playing by the "established rules," Musk's teams took a completely different approach. They started with those audacious, eyebrow-raising goals we talked about, like making electric vehicles mainstream or colonizing Mars, and then built every system around achieving those futures.

If you look under the hood of these companies, you'll find systems deliberately designed to make those "impossible" timelines possible. They've mastered what I call "strategic impatience"—a relentless drive to eliminate anything that doesn't directly serve the end goal.

Think about it. When your vision is to put humans on Mars, you can't afford to get caught up in "that's how we've always done it" thinking. Every process, every meeting, every decision gets measured against one simple question: Does this get us closer to our objective, or is it just organizational busywork?

Hard truth incoming... Most businesses get this exactly backward. They try to stretch their existing systems to reach bigger goals, instead of building new systems specifically engineered for those objectives. That's like trying to win a Formula 1 race in your daily commuter car; you might finish, but you're not going to break any records.

The key takeaway here isn't about copying Musk's specific approaches—it's about understanding that truly transformative results require systems built with those results in mind from day one. When you architect your operations around your vision (rather than trying to retrofit your vision into existing operations), what seemed impossible suddenly becomes inevitable.

Now, I can already hear some of you thinking, *Mike, this sounds like a lot of work. We're a lean team; we don't have time for all this measurement and analysis.* But honestly, the truth is you don't have time *not* to do this. The price of missed opportunities is too steep.

I'll share a story of a past client that perfectly illustrates this point (names changed to protect the ambitious). Susan ran a consulting firm that was doing "fine": about $800K annually with a small team. But she had a vision of hitting $5M within 24 months. Most people would have told her to slow down, to be "realistic."

Instead of pulling back on that goal, we helped her apply the Vision First Framework. The first thing we did? Completely ignored her current systems and started fresh with systems designed for a $5M company.

Here's where it gets interesting...

When we mapped out what a $5M operation *had* to look like (notice I said had to, not could), we discovered her current setup could maybe handle $1.5M at best. The systems just weren't built for that level of scale. This is what I call the "Infrastructure Gap"—when your operational foundation can't support your vision.

Some quick math showed she needed:

- 3x more qualified leads per month.
- 5x faster client onboarding process.
- 2x higher average client value.
- Systems that could handle 4x the current client load without adding proportional staff.

Most business owners would look at numbers like these and think "impossible." But remember what we covered in the Vision First Framework; we're not trying to stretch current systems. We're building new ones specifically engineered for these targets.

Susan's team started by designing their client acquisition system backward from their goal. Instead of asking, "How can we get more leads?" they asked, "What would a system that consistently delivers

50 qualified prospects per month look like?" (See the difference in thinking there?)

The results? In less than four months, they had:

- Automated 70% of their client onboarding.
- Created scalable delivery systems that reduced service time by 38%.
- Implemented a new pricing structure that doubled their average client value.
- Built a lead generation engine that could actually support their revenue goals.

And this is where it gets really good...

By month ten, they were on pace for $3.2M annually, not because they worked harder, but because they built systems sized for their vision rather than their current reality.

The lesson here isn't about the specific numbers. It's about understanding that when you build systems explicitly engineered for your desired future—not just optimized versions of your current processes—breakthrough results become possible.

Think about it this way: If I asked you to build a bridge to support 10,000 cars per day, you'd design it very differently than one meant for 100 cars. Business systems work the same way. The infrastructure needed for 10x growth isn't just a bigger version of what you're doing now; it's often fundamentally different.

This is why I'm constantly telling clients: Your systems are either multiplying your efforts or limiting your growth. There's no middle ground.

"Every system in your business is either built for where you already are or engineered for where you're going."

The question is: Which are yours?

LASER NOT FLASHLIGHT

Any leader with an IQ above 80 knows they need to prioritize. What many miss, though, is that prioritization isn't only about managing time, it's also about managing *energy*, which is one of our most precious resources.

Here's the reality: Time is finite—limited to the hours in a day and the number of days we're blessed to be here. Energy at the quantum level is infinite, but our human capacity to tap into and use that energy is not. Everything we achieve in this world happens within these two forces [Time x Energy].

Even for the most disciplined among us—I'm willing to bet that if we analyzed this aspect of your life right now, there's no less than one to two hours per day slipping between the cracks of inefficiency. In business, efficiency directly correlates to your impact.

Think about this: I know people quietly making tens of millions of dollars and changing lives while others are loudmouthing across social media, moving a million miles an hour, thirsting for attention, claiming to be experts, and never making any positive impact in their own lives, much less anyone else's.

My point is:

> *"Activity gives you the illusion of progress.*
> *Productivity leaves evidence."*

One of my favorite questions to ask clients is, "If you could only solve one problem that would fundamentally transform your business, what would it be?" Not what should be solved, or what could be solved, but what *must* be solved?"

This is where most business books get it wrong. They tell you to prioritize (obvious) but don't explain the physics of why it matters. When you diffuse your team's energy across multiple initiatives, you're not just dividing their time; you're dramatically reducing their power. A flashlight can illuminate a room, but a laser can cut through steel: same energy, a profoundly different impact.

As a visionary leader, your job is to ensure that all this innovation and experimentation is still moving you toward your ultimate vision, because every time you say "yes" to a new initiative, you're not just allocating resources—you're diffusing your organization's creative power.

Learning when to say "no" (even when it's a good idea) is a superpower you'll need to hone as a leader. Steve Jobs nailed this perfectly when he said, "I'm as proud of many of the things we haven't done as the things we have done. Innovation is saying no to a thousand things."

As a Systems-Thinking Visionary, your role transcends traditional leadership. You're not just an idea generator or decision-maker; you're an energy architect. Your systems should act like lenses, focusing your team's collective power toward breakthrough objectives rather than just managing daily operations.

Years ago, I created an ultra-simple system that provides instant priority recognition. It first helps you identify where your time and energy are being spent, then allows you to calibrate your focus toward the things that matter most and produce the most leverage.

The Color Code System is simple but powerful, and the best part is you don't need any expensive or complicated tech to implement it.

Go to SystemsThinkingVisionary.com/resources for a quick tutorial and downloadable tools.

Remember this: Every 15 minutes you spend planning and optimizing how you use your time and energy will produce a 10X or more return-on-effort (ROE). When you want to move more profitably and at a high pace, think laser, not flashlight.

TRIMMING THE FAT

When I audit a new client's systems, what we uncover usually shocks them. It's not uncommon to find 20% to 40% of their operational costs going to tools, processes, and roles that don't drive their vision forward. They're stuck in what I call the "Legacy Trap"—keeping things not because they serve the future but because they're remnants of the past.

Complexity compounds. Every system, process, or role you maintain creates drag on your entire operation. Think of it like running with weights strapped to your ankles—you can do it, but you're burning precious energy fighting unnecessary resistance.

The most dangerous complexities aren't the obvious ones. They hide in plain sight in those "reasonable" decisions that seemed right at the time but now act like organizational scar tissue, slowly restricting your company's ability to move and adapt.

Let me share a perfect example. Recently, I asked a founder to map out their client onboarding process. "It's pretty straightforward," he assured me. Once we actually documented it? Forty-seven distinct steps in the process—many existing solely because "that's how we've always done it." We cut it to 12 steps, and almost instantly client satisfaction went up because we eliminated the friction points that were actually hurting the experience.

This is where systems thinking becomes your secret weapon. Instead of just adding new solutions, you develop the clarity to spot what needs to be eliminated. *Sometimes, your most powerful move isn't building a new system; it's dismantling an old one.*

Think about quantum physics: a particle can't reach a higher energy state without releasing energy from its current state. Your business works the same way. You often need to let go of the structures that got you here to reach your next level.

In our next chapter, we'll explore how to make confident decisions in the face of complexity, and why traditional decision-making frameworks often fail. More importantly, you'll learn how to build a decision-making system that amplifies your natural intuition instead of fighting it.

Remember: What separates good visionaries from great ones isn't just what they build—it's what they have the courage to break down. Let's make that your competitive advantage.

QUESTIONS TO CONSIDER

1. Take a hard look at your current business systems. If you scaled 10X tomorrow, which systems would amplify your growth and which would break under pressure? What specific gaps exist between your vision and your operational infrastructure?

2. Think about your last three major initiatives. Did your systems accelerate or handicap their implementation? Where could you have eliminated complexity to achieve better results with less effort?

3. Using the Vision-First Framework we covered, identify one critical system in your business that's built for where you are rather than where you're going. What would that same system look like if it were engineered specifically for your 24-month vision?

4. Consider your feedback loops. Are you measuring what matters or what's convenient? What specific data points, if tracked, would fundamentally change how you make decisions?

5. Reflect on your "Legacy Trap" vulnerabilities. What processes or systems are you keeping purely out of habit or comfort? What would happen if you eliminated them entirely?

SIX

QUANTUM DECISION-MAKING
TOPIC: MAKING BETTER DECISIONS, FASTER

"The decisions you make today shape your tomorrow.
Make each decision with the clarity of where you want to go."
—Tony Robbins

MAKING BETTER DECISIONS, FASTER

Let's address something that's probably been frustrating you for a while. Despite all your experience with decision-making frameworks —the SWOT analysis, decision trees, and every other strategy tool out there—something still feels off. Maybe you've even got a favorite framework that's served you well. But here's what nobody's talking about: those tools were built for a different era.

Think about it. The pace of change, the technology, the interconnectedness of everything—we're not just dealing with more complexity, we're dealing with a fundamentally different kind of complexity.

I saw this play out recently during an intense strategy session with a CEO facing a crucial pivot decision. Markets shifting, competitors advancing, and millions in future revenue hanging in the balance. He had more data, more experience, and more expert opinions than ever before. The result? Complete paralysis.

With today's technology, we're not suffering from a lack of information; we're drowning in it. I call it "death by data." Being buried in spreadsheets and analytics can be just as crippling as flying blind. Maybe worse, because at least when you're flying blind, you know you need to rely on something deeper than just numbers.

This is where traditional decision-making frameworks get it completely wrong. They treat decision-making like a math problem —gather data, analyze options, and pick the "logical" choice. But if you're a visionary thinker, your mind doesn't work in neat, linear paths. It operates in patterns and possibilities.

I'm going to show you a fundamentally different approach—one that works with your visionary mind instead of against it. We're not throwing out analysis or ignoring data. Instead, we're going to integrate your natural pattern recognition abilities with systems thinking to make better decisions under pressure. More importantly, I'll show you how to turn what most people see as overwhelming complexity into your greatest advantage.

SEEING MULTIPLE FUTURES SIMULTANEOUSLY

Traditional decision-making would say: List the pros and cons, analyze the data, make the "logical" choice. But here's what I've learned working with visionary leaders—the biggest opportunities rarely look good on a spreadsheet.

I want to introduce you to a concept I call Quantum Decision-Making. And no, this isn't some woo-woo, pseudoscience nonsense. This is about applying cutting-edge concepts from quantum physics to revolutionize how you approach decisions in business and how they create ripple effects throughout your entire organization and beyond.

An excellent case study for this is Netflix's pivotal decision to shift from DVDs to streaming. A traditional pros/cons analysis would have likely killed the idea. The infrastructure wasn't ready.

The licensing costs were enormous. The existing business was still profitable.

But Reed Hastings, Co-Founder of Netflix, saw something deeper—patterns indicating where entertainment was heading. He understood that this wasn't just a tactical decision about delivery methods. It was about the future of how humans would consume content.

Here's how to develop this superpower:

First, stop trying to make perfect decisions. Instead, explore multiple possible futures simultaneously. When facing a big decision, I map out at least four wildly different scenarios, including ones that seem unlikely at first. Traditional decision-making asks, "Should we do A or B?" whereas Quantum Decision-Making asks, "How might A and B (and C and D) play out in different scenarios?"

When Netflix faced its streaming decision, they didn't only evaluate "DVDs versus streaming." They asked:

- What if we went all-in on streaming?
- What if we maintained both services?
- What if streaming technology isn't ready yet?
- What if someone else beats us to market?

By holding all these possibilities in mind simultaneously, they spotted opportunities and risks that a simple yes/no decision would have missed.

This goes way beyond just brainstorming random ideas. It's about seeing how different possibilities connect and influence each other. Each potential decision creates ripple effects throughout your business. Your job is to spot those ripples before they become waves.

Here's how to put this into practice today:

1. Write down your current big decision.
2. Force yourself to imagine four radically different ways forward.

3. For each option, ask: "If we did this, what else would change in our business?"
4. Look for patterns and connections between the scenarios.
5. Pay attention to your team's reactions. Their energy often reveals hidden insights.

An important distinction I want to highlight here is that your instincts as a visionary aren't random. As your entrepreneurial and life experiences increase, that "gut feeling" can become more and more finely tuned into an opportunity-seeking radar. Now don't get me wrong, I'm not suggesting abandoning analysis or ignoring data. But as time goes by, you'll more and more be able to expand your vision to see possibilities that traditional decision-making might miss, patterns too complex for conscious analysis.

Your most powerful decisions will come from combining rigorous analysis with pattern recognition. That's how you spot opportunities others miss and make bold moves with confidence.

Ready to test this out? Take one significant decision you're facing right now and map out your four scenarios. You might be surprised at what patterns emerge.

PUTTING IT ALL TOGETHER: A PRACTICAL EXAMPLE

Let's see how this works in practice. Here's how Hilary, a software CEO client, used this framework to make a crucial decision about international expansion:

1. Instead of asking, "Should we expand to Europe?" she explored four radically different scenarios that they could take:
   o Full expansion right now
   o Gradual country-by-country approach
   o Strategic partnerships
   o Remote-first presence

2. She then mapped the major connections between each option, things like:
   ○ Team culture (how will this impact our team?)
   ○ Product development (how will this impact R&D?)
   ○ Customer support (how will this impact client experience?)
   ○ Financial resources (how will this impact cash flow?)

3. As she was going through this process, she reported how just exploring expansion had already begun to cause noticeable ripple effects:
   ○ Her team felt reenergized with new possibilities.
   ○ She attracted interest from potential partners she'd never considered.
   ○ The team identified internal capabilities they hadn't recognized.

4. This exploration process soon revealed an unexpected path: starting with a small European hub that could serve multiple countries while maintaining its company culture.

The result was a successful expansion that avoided the usual pitfalls while creating unexpected opportunities.

REFRAMING FAILURE

Let's talk about failure for a moment. In his book *Failing Forward: Turning Mistakes Into Stepping Stones for Success*, John C. Maxwell popularized the concept of "failing forward." Maxwell emphasizes the importance of viewing failure as an opportunity for growth and learning rather than something to be avoided. The idea is that by embracing failure and learning from it, we can make progress and eventually succeed.

Now, while I agree with the general premise and count it as valuable wisdom, what if we've been thinking about the entire process in a way that puts too much emphasis on failure?

Here's what I mean: The concept of "failure" is built on a flawed assumption. It presumes that success is a destination rather than a calibration process.

I know what you're thinking. "Mike, isn't this just semantics? Why does it matter what we call it?" Bear with me here because this shift in thinking is more than just wordplay. I'm talking about fundamentally changing how you approach your goals and decision-making process.

Think about it this way: When we talk about "failure," there's this implication of finality. Something went wrong, and now we need to recover. But things are rarely that black and white. What if every misstep, every setback, wasn't a failure at all, but simply an iteration that moves you closer to your goal?

For perspective, when a pilot is navigating through storm systems, every air current becomes intelligence, every pocket of turbulence a data point. The constant stream of adjustments isn't correcting previous mistakes—it's real-time adaptation to an ever-evolving reality. The difference between excellence and mediocrity isn't in avoiding the need to adjust, but in how quickly and precisely those adjustments translate into forward progress.

Let's put this into context for business. Low user adoption? That's not a failure; it's feedback. It's telling us something about our product-market fit. Hemorrhaging money? That's not a failure; it's information about our business model and pricing strategy. Each of these "failures" is actually a crucial data point guiding us toward success.

Now, let's break down why this "calibration" mindset is so powerful:

First, it removes the emotional weight of failure. When we fail, it can feel deeply personal. We didn't meet expectations, and we might start doubting ourselves. But calibration is emotionally neutral. It's solely focused on understanding the mechanics of progress.

Early in my consulting career, I was working with a founder who was paralyzed by an important product decision. "Mike," he said, "I can't afford to get this wrong. One bad move and we're done."

This mindset was actually his biggest threat, *not the decision itself*. He was so focused on avoiding failure that he couldn't see the opportunity cost of not deciding. Here's the truth about high-stakes decisions:

"The biggest risk isn't making the wrong choice.
It's taking too long to make any choice at all."

Think about Amazon's early decision to expand beyond books. If Jeff Bezos had waited for "perfect" data, someone else would almost certainly dominate e-commerce today. Instead, he understood that every decision is a learning opportunity.

This brings us to what I call "Decision Velocity"—the speed at which you can make, learn from, and adjust decisions. In today's fast-moving markets, this is often more important than making the "perfect" choice.

Here's how to increase your Decision Velocity:

Start viewing decisions as experiments rather than final verdicts. When I work with clients, we rarely talk about failure. Instead, we ask: "What did this decision teach us?"

One of our clients recently faced a decision about entering a new market. Instead of spending months analyzing every possibility, they ran three small-scale tests simultaneously. Each "mini-failure" provided insights that eventually led to a breakthrough approach no competitor had tried.

The key is to make reversible decisions where possible. Ask yourself: "If this doesn't work, how easily can we pivot?" Some decisions are truly irreversible, but most aren't. We just treat them that way out of fear.

Think like a scientist running experiments. Each decision is a hypothesis to test:

- "I believe this new feature will increase retention..."
- "I think this pricing model will attract enterprise clients..."
- "This marketing channel should reach our ideal customers..."

Better decisions do come from better analysis, but what I've learned after years of working with visionary leaders is that great decisions don't start with better analysis; they start with better questions.

THE POWER OF BETTER QUESTIONS

Do you know what consistently separates great decisions from mediocre ones? It's not the analysis—it's the questions asked before the analysis even starts:

"The quality of your questions determines the quality of your decisions, which ultimately shapes the reality of your business."

Most leaders jump straight to "What should we do?" But that's like trying to solve a maze from the middle. The real breakthroughs come from asking better questions up-front.

Here's a recent example from one of our clients. They were stuck deciding between expanding their product line or doubling down on their core offer. But they were asking the wrong question. Instead of "Which path should we take?" we shifted to "What problem are we actually trying to solve?"

This simple reframe revealed something crucial—their real challenge wasn't about product strategy at all. *It was about customer retention.* This clarity led to a solution they hadn't even considered: creating a customer success division that ended up driving more growth than a new product line would have.

When you're facing a high-stakes decision, here are three powerful questions that can transform your thinking:

"What problem am I actually trying to solve?"

Often, you're solving the wrong problem brilliantly. Get clear on the real issue first.

"What would make this decision irrelevant?"

This is my favorite question for breaking through mental blocks. One client realized their pricing decision didn't matter because they were selling to the wrong customer segment entirely.

"What does my future self wish I had considered?"

This creates emotional distance and helps you spot long-term implications you might miss otherwise.

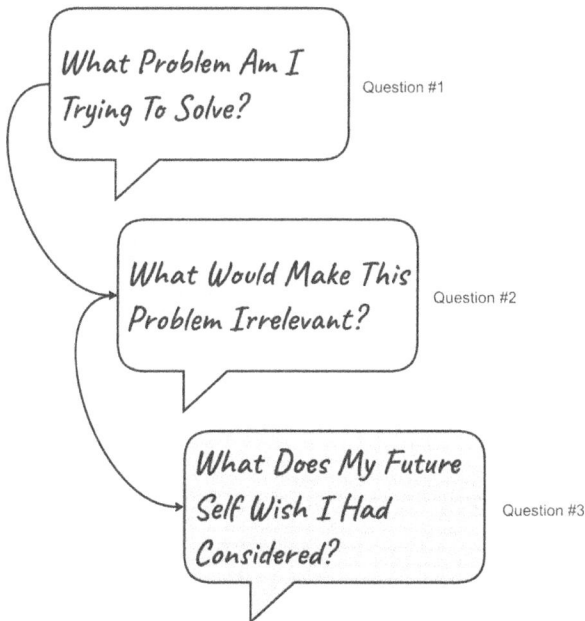

What Problem Am I Trying To Solve?   Question #1

What Would Make This Problem Irrelevant?   Question #2

What Does My Future Self Wish I Had Considered?   Question #3

This is precisely where most decision-making advice stops. But there's actually one more crucial element: the questions you ask *after* making the decision. This is where real learning happens.

Instead of asking, "Did this work?" try asking, "What did this teach us that we couldn't have known before?" "What new possibilities does this open up?" "What patterns are we seeing that could inform our next move?"

Write this down manually, pen to paper to embed it into your brain:

The quality of your questions determines the quality of your decisions. Start asking higher-quality questions, and you'll naturally make higher-quality choices.

Here's a powerful realization that I wish I had learned earlier in my career and one that has changed how I coach leaders. In every major success story I've witnessed, the game-changing decision wasn't achieved by having perfect information. It was about having the confidence to act on subtle patterns that others missed.

A classic example of this is how Steve Jobs made the radical decision to open Apple retail stores when everyone said they would fail. He wasn't just guessing; he was pattern matching. He saw how luxury brands created experiences, not just products. He understood that controlling the customer experience was worth more than the obvious retail risks.

This is the level of decision-making you're capable of, and here's your action plan on how to do it. For your next big decision:

- Map out multiple possibilities (even unlikely ones).
- Look for patterns and connections others might miss.
- Move fast, but make it reversible where possible.
- Ask better questions before and after.
- Learn from the results, regardless of the outcome.

The ability to make bold decisions quickly and learn from the data and feedback you get in return is your real competitive advantage.

In the next chapter, we'll explore how to build and lead teams that can execute these decisions at speed.

I want to ease your mind on this topic... Your future success does not require that you make perfect choices. It hinges on your confidence and capability to make increasingly better decisions, faster, over time. Start applying these principles that we've covered here, and watch how your decision-making transforms from a source of stress to a source of strength.

QUESTIONS TO CONSIDER

1. Think about the most pressing decision on your desk right now. Map out four radically different scenarios using the Quantum Decision-Making framework we covered. What unexpected patterns or opportunities emerge when you hold all these possibilities in mind simultaneously?

2. Consider your last three major business "calibrations" (what others might call failures). What systemic patterns do they reveal about your decision-making process? More importantly, what would these patterns tell your future self about the decisions you're facing today?

3. Audit your current decision velocity. Are you making reversible decisions quickly enough to generate learning opportunities, or are you treating every choice like it's permanent? What specific systems could you put in place to increase your speed while maintaining quality?

4. Look at the questions you typically ask before making big decisions. Are they truly serving your vision, or are they

just recycled business school frameworks? What happens when you apply the three transformative questions we covered to your current biggest challenge?

5. Examine a competitor's recent major decision that surprised you. Using the pattern recognition principles we discussed, what subtle market signals might they have seen that you missed? How could this insight change your approach to reading market patterns?

SEVEN
ENGINEERING EXCELLENCE
TOPIC: CULTIVATING A HIGH-PERFORMANCE TEAM CULTURE

"The greatest leaders are not those who inspire others to follow them, but those who inspire others to lead."
—John Quincy Adams

CULTIVATING A HIGH-PERFORMANCE TEAM CULTURE

Time for some radical honesty about a challenge that even exceptional leaders rarely discuss openly. You've got world-changing ideas, you're well into the process of mastering systems thinking by working through the chapters of this book, and you're ready to revolutionize your industry.

But there's still one challenge that might be keeping you up at night: leading your team.

If so, you're certainly not alone, but let me share something that might surprise you: Some of the most brilliant visionaries I've worked with were unknowingly holding their teams back. Not because they lacked great ideas or leadership skills but because they were trying to create teams in their image.

In the last chapter, we developed your ability to make bold decisions by recognizing patterns others miss. But here's where most visionaries get stuck—they try to teach everyone on their team to see those same patterns. That's like trying to teach a fish to climb a tree. Instead of forcing everyone to think like you, what if you could create an environment where different types of thinking work in harmony?

"Great visionaries don't showcase their genius. They build stages where others' genius performs."

THE VISIONARY'S ECOSYSTEM

When it comes to developing truly world-class organizations, I find it helps to imagine your team as a complex ecosystem, like a coral reef. Each member is a unique species, interdependent yet distinct.

When I first share this analogy with clients, they often nod politely but miss the profound implication of what this actually means: In nature, it's the *diversity of species* that creates resilience. A monoculture might look organized, but it's incredibly fragile.

Your role as a visionary leader is to create the conditions where this ecosystem thrives, where each individual can adapt, grow, and contribute to the whole in ways that benefit both them as an individual and the project at hand.

"This all sounds great, Mike, but if you were a fly on the wall at one of our team meetings, you'd quickly see that everyone seems to be talking different languages."

As a visionary leader, your ability to recognize and adapt to different thinking styles is crucial. Understanding these four archetypes of the Visionary's Ecosystem will help you communicate more effectively and build better systems. Think of them as different programming languages; to be a truly effective Systems-Thinking Visionary, you need to be fluent in all of them.

Let's break down what you're likely to encounter and how to speak their language:

1. The Pattern Seers (Visionaries)

- Natural ability to spot trends and opportunities.
- Think in possibilities and potential.
- Excel at connecting seemingly unrelated dots.
- Often frustrated by details and routine.

Your challenge: Create systems to channel multiple visionary perspectives without losing focus.
Your approach: Build frameworks that turn competing visions into complementary insights.

2. The Systems Architects (Integrators)

- Natural ability to create order from chaos.
- Think in processes and frameworks.
- Excel at turning vision into repeatable systems.
- Often frustrated by constant change and pivots.

Your challenge: Learn to communicate vision in terms of systematic components.
Your approach: Break down your ideas into clear, mappable elements they can systematize.

3. The Momentum Builders (Executors)

- Natural ability to get things done.
- Think in concrete steps and timelines.
- Excel at maintaining pace and progress.
- Often frustrated by unclear priorities or shifting goals.

Your challenge: Translate your vision into actionable steps.
Your approach: Create clear success metrics and milestone markers.

4. The Bridge Builders (Translators)

- Natural ability to speak multiple "languages".
- Think in connections and relationships.
- Excel at helping different types work together.
- Often frustrated by siloed thinking or communication barriers.

Your challenge: Use their insights to improve your systems.
Your approach: Learn from how they translate between different thinking styles.

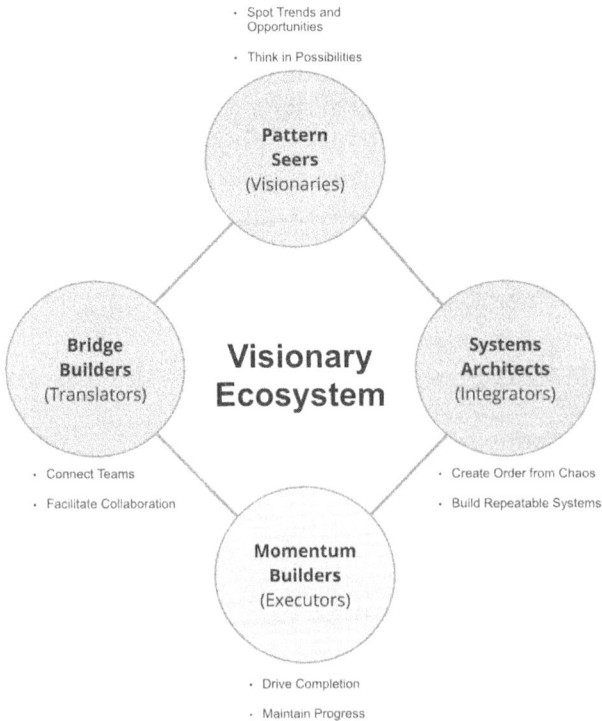

Instead of trying to force your technical team to think and talk like salespeople (or vice versa), you simply need to provide structured ways for different mindsets to communicate and collaborate.

There are plenty of ways to achieve this, but one of my favorites is to provide an opportunity for each department to update their peers on the top three risks and top three developments in their respective departments. Just this one practice alone can unlock monumental progress and new ideas. The cross-pollination of ideas can significantly bolster team synergy and a deeper, more meaningful understanding of how their individual efforts contribute to the company as a whole.

A simple but powerful example:

On Mondays and Fridays, we have leaders from Client Services attend the Sales team's daily morning huddle. This provides a perfect opportunity for the team members who are engaging with clients on a daily basis to provide a feedback loop to the sales team with success stories and other insights about the client experience that they can later refer to when speaking to other prospects who may relate to that specific example.

Regardless of how you decide to implement this level of commu-nication, the goal is the same—create transparency between depart-ments. Be sure that the right-hand knows what the left hand is doing.

If Marketing is going to launch a new product, communicate those details with the frontline support team *in advance* so that they are fully up to speed on the product and the likely expectations of the customers purchasing it. If Client Services begins to spot a trend in retention with a particular subset of clients, relay that intel to the Sales team so they can adjust focus and optimize toward the type of customer most likely to benefit from the services being provided.

Ultimately, we want to curate an environment where shared information and collaboration provide visionaries with a place to share ideas, patterns, and possibilities, for executors to identify and measure clear success metrics, and for system thinkers to map out interconnections and opportunities to increase efficiency.

UNLEASHING COLLECTIVE GENIUS

Do you ever find yourself thinking that if you want something done right, you need to do it yourself? After all, who understands your vision better than you do, right?!

This mindset is a fast track to overwhelm and, ironically, one of the biggest obstacles to realizing your vision. The art of effective delegation is much more than just offloading tasks—it means empowering your teams, scaling your impact, and freeing your mind to focus on what truly matters.

Imagine laying out all your responsibilities on a giant table. Now, step back and look at this landscape of tasks with a critical eye. Which of these truly requires your unique skills and vision? Which are time-consuming but don't leverage your specific expertise? Working through this exercise will do more than just help identify what to delegate—it'll also realign your mind with your role as a visionary leader.

A powerful tool for this analysis is the Eisenhower Matrix. Start by drawing a square divided into four quadrants: urgent and important, important but not urgent, urgent but not important, and neither urgent nor important.

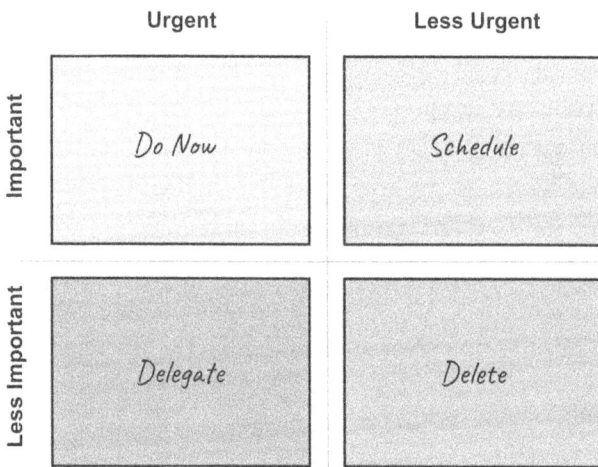

	Urgent	Less Urgent
Important	Do Now	Schedule
Less Important	Delegate	Delete

As you categorize your tasks into these four quadrants, you'll likely find that many items falling into the "urgent but not important" category are prime candidates for delegation.

Once you've identified the appropriate tasks to move off your plate, the next critical step is matching the right task to the right person at the right time. This is where many leaders falter, treating delegation as a simple handoff rather than a strategic process.

To excel at this matchmaking, you need to develop a deep understanding of your team. Beyond just their current skills and capacities, you need to consider their potential, their career aspirations, and even their work styles. This level of insight doesn't happen overnight —it requires intentional effort and genuine interest in your team member's own development.

Most leaders either overcomplicate delegation or avoid it altogether and try to strong-arm everything themselves. If either scenario feels relatable, I want to share a delegation framework that I think you'll find straightforward but powerful:

First, paint the bigger picture. Your team needs to understand why this matters, not just what needs to get done. When they see how their piece fits into the larger vision, they'll make better decisions without constantly checking in with you.

Next, get crystal clear on what winning actually looks like; don't assume their definition is the same as yours. This is where many leaders drop the ball... they assume their team can read their mind about expectations. Basic concept? Sure, but don't be surprised at how easily this gets overlooked when the pressure is on, and things are happening fast.

Here's a game-changer that can transform your capacity as a leader: explicitly define their decision-making authority. Are they empowered to spend money? Make judgment calls? Bring in other team members? Make it black and white.

Give them a clear inventory of their resources—what tools, budget, and support can they tap into? Nothing kills momentum faster than your team getting stuck because they didn't know what was available to them.

The truth is that effective delegation is about multiplying your impact. When done right, you're building a team that can execute your vision even when you're not in the room. Isn't that what you really want? A team that operates as an extension of your vision, not just a group waiting for orders?

Start implementing this framework, and watch how quickly your team steps up to own their results.

MONITORING WITHOUT MICROMANAGING

Alright, great—you're ready to start leveraging your team's abilities better. One of the biggest challenges visionary leaders face when delegating is finding the right balance between oversight and autonomy. They know they need to step back, but they're worried about losing control. Sound familiar? The key is to implement systems that provide visibility without requiring constant intervention.

Consider implementing a tiered review system. This approach recognizes that not all projects require the same level of oversight. Imagine a spectrum of autonomy, with three distinct levels:

1. **High autonomy tasks:** Assignments where you trust your team member to handle the entire process, and you'll only review the prelaunch gameplan and the final output.

2. **Moderate oversight tasks:** For these, you might include a couple of additional check-ins at key milestones to review progress and consider pivots if needed.

3. **Close guidance tasks:** This level of oversight should be used sparingly, typically for new team members or particularly complex or high-stakes projects.

High Autonomy	Moderate Oversight	Close Guidance
(2 Touch Points)	(4 Touch Points)	(8+ Touch Points)

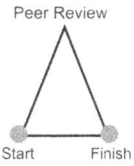

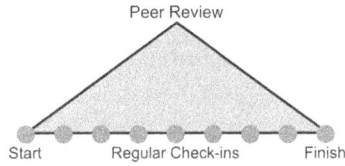

Peer Review | Peer Review | Peer Review

Start Finish | Start Milestones Finish | Start Regular Check-ins Finish

The beauty of this tiered system is its flexibility. As your team members grow in skills and confidence, you can gradually move tasks up the autonomy spectrum, freeing up more of your time and mental energy.

CONTINUOUS IMPROVEMENT

It should go without saying that delegation isn't a "set it and forget it" process. It's a dynamic, evolving practice that requires constant refinement. Each time you delegate a task, you have the chance to learn, grow, and improve the entire delegation process.

One of the most powerful tools you can apply to your business, especially with high-leverage projects and initiatives that have the potential for big payoffs, is the "after-action review." Don't let the fancy name fool you—it's simply sitting down with your team after completing a project and having an honest conversation about what happened.

Think about your last big project. When it wrapped up, did you immediately jump into the next thing? Most leaders do. But what separates the good from the great is taking time to learn from what just happened (ah, yes, more feedback loops).

Get your team together and start with the basics: What were we trying to accomplish? What actually happened? Having everyone share their perspective is pure gold. You'll be amazed at what comes up when you create a safe space for honest feedback.

The key is to focus on learning, not blame. When something worked well, figure out why so you can repeat it. When something goes sideways, treat it as valuable information about what to adjust next time.

I've seen too many leaders skip this part because they think they don't have time. But trust me, this investment pays massive dividends.

Make sure you let this concept sink in because it's subtle, but it carries a high level of potency when applied correctly.

"The goal in business is not just to complete the project at hand—it's to build a team that gets stronger and more capable with every task they tackle."

That only happens when you create an environment where learning is baked into the process.

The best part is that this isn't complicated stuff. After every major project, ask three simple questions:

1. What worked? (So we can do more of it.)
2. What didn't? (So we can fix it.)
3. What could we do differently next time? (i.e., apply 1 and 2.)

But here's where most leaders miss the boat completely... they never ask their team about the delegation process itself. Big mistake.

Your team has insights you need to hear. Maybe they need more clarity up front. Maybe there's a tool that could make everything smoother. Maybe there's a communication bottleneck you don't even know about.

I'll tell you a quick story: years ago, I had a client whose entire team was struggling with delegation. Turns out, after actually asking them, the issue wasn't the tasks at all; it was simply that nobody knew their spending limits. One simple clarity fix changed everything.

The point is, when you treat delegation as a two-way learning process, your team gets stronger, you get better at letting go, and suddenly you have the mental space to focus on the big-picture stuff that only you can do.

Listen, I get that all of this might sound like a lot of work. But the leaders who invest time in mastering delegation end up with way more time and energy to focus on growth. The ones who don't? They stay stuck playing whack-a-mole with endless tasks and problems.

The beautiful thing about this approach is that it creates a virtuous cycle. Your team learns faster. They take more initiative. They start solving problems before they even reach your desk. Before you know it, they're operating at a level you never thought possible.

And let me tell you, there's nothing quite like the feeling of watching your team truly excel without needing you to hold their hand every step of the way.

Remember: Every time you delegate a task, you're not just getting something off your plate; you're investing in your team's growth and your company's future.

Start small if you need to. Pick one project, implement these feedback loops, review practices in your business, and watch what happens. I promise you'll never look at delegation the same way again.

One last suggestion here before we move on from this topic. The best leaders don't just delegate tasks, they delegate authority. They create what I call "decision zones" where their team knows exactly what calls they can make on their own.

Think about it. What's the point of delegating if your team still has to come to you for every little decision? That's not delegation—that's just creating extra steps.

When you delegate a project, be crystal clear about:

- What decisions they can make on their own.
- What spending authority they have.
- When they need to loop you in.
- Who else they can involve.

Before we wrap up this chapter, here's something worth internalizing. Read it a couple of times to make sure it sinks in:

"Your team's performance in your absence reveals far more about your leadership than their achievements under your direct guidance."

Most visionary leaders intellectually understand this concept, but they struggle with the execution. Why? Because letting go feels like losing control. But control is actually an illusion that's holding you back from your next level of impact.

Let me be direct: If your business can't thrive without your constant involvement, you haven't built a business—you've built a job. And a demanding one at that. True visionary leadership means building systems and teams that make you progressively less necessary for daily operations.

Here's your action plan:

1. Identify one key decision you're currently making that your team could own.
2. Create clear success criteria for that decision.
3. Explicitly delegate both the authority and responsibility.
4. Force yourself to stay out of the process unless explicitly asked.
5. Document what you learn from the experience.

In our next chapter on "Synergistic Scaling," you'll discover why this foundation of empowered teams and robust systems means the difference between hitting a ceiling and breaking through to your next level of growth.

Before we jump into it, though, take a moment now to reflect on the questions below. Your answers will highlight specific opportunities to strengthen your team culture and prepare the foundation for your next phase of growth.

QUESTIONS TO CONSIDER

1. Using the Visionary's Ecosystem framework, identify which of the four archetypes (Pattern Seers, Systems Architects, Momentum Builders, Bridge Builders) are currently missing or underutilized in your organization. What specific gaps in your team's capabilities are these missing pieces creating?

2. Think about your most recent "bottleneck moment." Was it truly about capability, or was it about your resistance to delegation? Map out one process where you could implement the tiered review system we discussed, and detail exactly what "high autonomy" would look like for that process.

3. Look at your last three major team conflicts. Were they really about the issues at hand, or about different thinking styles clashing? How could you use the communication frameworks we covered to turn these friction points into opportunities for synthesis?

4. Consider your current delegation practices. Are you truly delegating authority or just tasks? What specific "decision zones" could you establish this week that would empower your team while maintaining appropriate oversight through the systems we discussed?

5. Audit your last month of team interactions. How often did you step in to "help" versus let your team struggle through to their own solutions? What systems could you put in place to make yourself progressively less necessary while ensuring quality remains high?

EIGHT
SYNERGISTIC SCALING
TOPIC: GROWING WITHOUT BREAKING

"The art of scaling isn't in growing bigger, but in growing stronger. Like a tree, each ring of growth should reinforce your core, not dilute it."
—Naval Ravikant

GROWING WITHOUT BREAKING

I see this pattern play out with scary predictability...

A visionary builds something remarkable—proven products, strong revenue, and talented teams. All the pieces are there. But they stay stuck at their current level, fighting the same battles over and over instead of breaking through to the next phase of growth.

The mistake? Treating scaling like a simple math problem—do more of what's working, just bigger. But real scaling isn't about doing more; it requires systematically upgrading your business's capacity for growth. Think quantum leaps, not linear steps. The systems that worked brilliantly at $1M will actively hold you back at $10M. The strategies that got you to $10M will cripple you at $100M.

In this chapter, we're going to break down exactly how to build a business that's engineered for continuous expansion. More importantly, you'll learn how to do it without sacrificing the vision and values that got you here.

So, strap in. We're about to put your systems-thinking skills to the ultimate test. I promise you this: the view from the top will be worth every step of the climb.

Let's start by examining what I call the DNA of Scalability—the core elements that determine whether your business can grow sustainably or if it's destined to hit a ceiling.

THE 5 GROWTH CODES: DNA OF SCALABILITY

When it comes to scaling, not all parts of your business are created equal. Like stretching a rubber band—some areas expand smoothly, while others snap under pressure. The key is to identify which elements of your business have scalability woven into their very DNA.

This is where many stumble. They try to scale everything simultaneously, treating each part of their business as equally expandable.

Instead of this brute force approach, let's implement what I call the Scalability DNA Test.

Growth Code #1: Look for Scale-Ready Systems

These have three distinct characteristics:

- They become more valuable as they grow.
- They can expand without proportional resource increases.
- They maintain or improve quality at scale.

Scale-Ready vs Non-Scale-Ready Systems

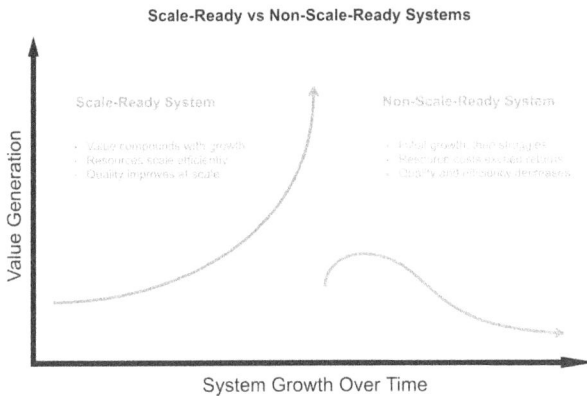

If you can verify these are in place, you're likely looking at a scalable component of your business.

Netflix's streaming service is a perfect example. Each new subscriber makes their recommendation engine smarter, their negotiating power stronger, and their content budget bigger. The core system actually improves as it gets bigger.

I can already feel some of you now, "Yeah, well, that's great, Mike, but I'm not Netflix. In my business, clients expect me to be involved. We're a much higher-touch business."

Despite common belief, even bespoke "done-for-you" services—businesses that seem inherently resistant to scaling—can be engineered for growth. Let me share a story that transformed how I learned to think about this...

I was working with a high-end interior design firm that initially seemed impossible to scale. Every project required the founder's creative vision, every client expected personal attention, and quality control was a constant challenge. Classic signs of a business trapped by its own success.

But when we dug deeper into their Scalability DNA, we spotted something promising. While the creative direction didn't scale, the *systems* around it could. So we immediately built frameworks that supported growth without compromising core values.

Here's what we did:

- They systematized 80% of their operations (client onboarding, project management, and vendor relationships). Regardless of the project and the client's needs, there were multiple steps that every client needed to do when first initiating a project. We simplified and systematized each of these steps.

- Created design templates and guidelines that captured the founder's vision. This drastically reduced the amount of back-and-forth communication that was required with clients. By referencing the materials, clients could navigate the decision-making processes more efficiently and effectively on their own.

- Built training systems that could reliably reproduce their quality standards. Anything that didn't absolutely need to be done by the founder was allocated to team members with step-by-step instructions and methods for verifying quality standards and client experience.

They went from handling eight projects a year to over forty while increasing their customer satisfaction scores. The founder went from being involved in every decision to only weighing in on key creative directions.

This project revealed a powerful truth about scaling: To grow bigger, you often need to narrow your focus. It sounds counterintuitive, but I've seen this principle transform businesses across every industry I've consulted in.

We can look at Amazon again as an example. They didn't start by selling everything. They mastered selling books first. Only after their systems were rock-solid did they expand. Each new category was built on proven systems, not a complete reinvention.

This brings me to a critical nuance in building businesses. The challenge isn't so much in identifying what scales; it's understanding the *sequence* of scaling. Knowing what to expand in what order.

Getting this sequence right is the difference between sustainable growth and chaotic expansion.

Growth Code #2: Identifying Quantum Leap Potential

Here's where systems thinking becomes your secret weapon. Most leaders look for growth in obvious places—more sales, more staff, and more locations. But quantum thinking reveals opportunities for exponential growth that most miss entirely.

Let me connect this to something we covered earlier about pattern recognition. In quantum physics, particles don't gradually climb an energy ladder; they can leap from one state to another without touching the middle rungs. Your business can do the same thing, but only if you build systems designed for these leaps.

Airbnb nailed this. Instead of thinking linearly ("let's add more properties"), they engineered a self-reinforcing system where every new component multiplied the value of existing ones. Each new host made the platform more valuable for guests, which attracted more guests, which attracted more hosts.

This is precisely where most visionaries miss their biggest opportunities. They're so focused on scaling what works that they miss chances to transform how their entire system operates.

Let me show you what this looks like in practice. During a recent strategy session, a client was convinced they needed to double their support team to handle growth. Classic linear thinking: More Clients = More Team = Linear Growth.

But when we applied systems-thinking to their challenge, we spotted something far more powerful. Their entire onboarding process could be transformed into a self-optimizing system that would not only handle unlimited customers but actually deliver a better experience with each new client.

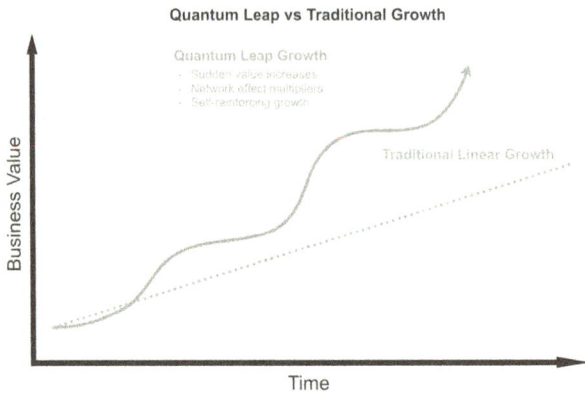

Quantum Leap vs Traditional Growth

When looking for Quantum Leap Potential:

- Think feedback loops, not linear paths. One of my clients transformed their referral system from a simple "thank you" into what I call a "Success Sharing System." They gave clients specific tools and frameworks to share their wins. The result? Each satisfied client now brings in an average of two new clients, who each bring in two more.
- Sometimes the smallest system change creates the biggest ripple effect. We helped a client redesign their sales response protocol, cutting initial contact time from two hours to five minutes. Just this one tweak doubled their conversion rate because they were catching prospects in their moment of peak interest. The system change took less than a day to implement but transformed their entire sales trajectory.

These opportunities already exist in your business right now. But you won't spot them if you're wearing the same glasses you've always worn. Sometimes, the biggest breakthroughs come from importing ideas from completely different industries or challenging your most basic assumptions about how things "should" work.

Quantum leaps rarely come from doing more of what already works. They come from fundamentally reimagining what's possible.

Growth Code #3: Keeping Your Vision Sharp While Scaling

Here's a truth that most visionaries learn the hard way: The faster you grow, the easier it is to lose sight of your vision. Like driving a race car, the faster you go, the further ahead you need to look, and the more crucial your systems become.

I can't tell you how many times I've watched businesses scale themselves right past their purpose. They hit their revenue targets but wake up one day running a company they never wanted to build.

Let me show you how to engineer this alignment:

First, strip away the PR version of your vision and get to its core operating system.

For every growth opportunity, your system needs to answer these questions:

- Does this create a multiplicative or just additive impact?
- Will this strengthen or dilute our vision at 10X scale?
- Does this move us closer to or further from our ultimate mission?

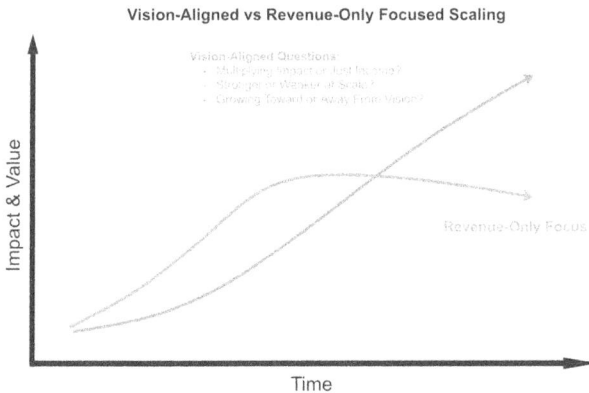

Vision-Aligned vs Revenue-Only Focused Scaling

Here's a perfect example: A few years ago, one of my clients who runs a high-end speaker training company was presented with what seemed like a golden opportunity—creating a mass-market digital product. The revenue projections certainly caught their attention.

But when we ran it through their vision-alignment system, we quickly saw that this "opportunity" would actually fragment their focus and weaken their position with the elite clients they truly wanted to serve.

Instead of chasing quick revenue, they rebuilt their systems to scale their high-touch programs more efficiently. Yes, they grew slower initially. However, by staying aligned with their vision, they created more value and commanded higher prices than they ever could have with the mass-market approach.

Growth Code #4: Values Stress Test

Now, imagine this element of your business growing 10x, 100x, or even 1000x. Stop at each level of growth, and ask yourself:

- Does this amplify or dilute our core values?
- Are we still serving our intended audience, just on a larger scale?
- Are we building what we set out to build, just bigger, or something entirely different?

To conceptualize this stress test concept, take Etsy, the e-commerce platform, which specializes in selling handmade goods and crafts. As they scaled, they had to constantly check whether their growth was still supporting their vision of empowering small, independent creators. When they started allowing manufactured goods on their platform to fuel growth, they faced significant backlash from their community who felt this diluted Etsy's core values. This decision, while potentially profitable in the short term, risked undermining the very essence that made Etsy unique and beloved by its core community of artisans and craft enthusiasts.

Values Stress Test at Scale

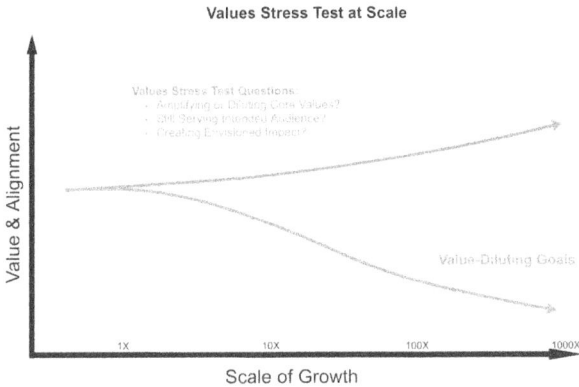

Scale of Growth

The companies that scale successfully don't just protect their values—they build systems that make their values stronger at scale. The $1.50 hot dog combo at Costco is a well-known example of their commitment to delivering value to their customers.

Costco's co-founder, Jim Sinegal, introduced the $1.50 hot dog and soda combo in 1985. Despite inflation and rising costs over the years, the price has remained unchanged. In a famous exchange, current Costco CEO Craig Jelinek reportedly suggested raising the price to reflect increasing costs. Sinegal's response was direct and now legendary: "If you raise the price of the hot dog, I will kill you." He then added, "Figure it out."

Costco took this challenge seriously and made operational changes to ensure the combo remained affordable. For example, they stopped outsourcing the production of their hot dogs and built their own manufacturing facilities to reduce costs and maintain control over pricing.

This anecdote has become a symbol of Costco's commitment to delivering consistent value to its members and refusing to compromise on certain principles, even in the face of financial pressure.

Growth Code #5: Synergistic Flywheels

Let me show you something that transformed how I think about scale. It's not uncommon for leaders to approach growth like they're building separate skyscrapers, focusing on one tower at a time. Treating individual departments or service tiers as separate entities. What I've learned studying companies like Tesla is that real scale comes from building interconnected systems that strengthen each other automatically.

There are plenty of examples out there, but Tesla's story illustrates this perfectly. Elon Musk and his team didn't just set out to build electric cars. They engineered an entire ecosystem where every component naturally accelerates the others' growth.

Every new Tesla on the road creates a natural demand for their Supercharger network. Each new charging station makes Tesla vehicles more practical for potential buyers. As their charging network expands, they gather invaluable data about driving patterns and energy usage, which helps them optimize both vehicle design and station placement.

Then there's their energy storage business. The Powerwall and Powerpack systems share the same core battery technology as their vehicles. When they improve battery efficiency for cars, those advances automatically enhance their storage products. Higher production volumes across all product lines drive down costs throughout the entire ecosystem.

When you look closely, you'll see that their battery technology forms the backbone of everything. Advances in any area cascade through their entire system. Better batteries mean improved vehicles, more efficient charging stations, and more powerful storage solutions. Each improvement multiplies across its whole ecosystem while pushing forward its mission of accelerating the world's transition to sustainable energy.

Tesla Case Study: Synergistic Growth Effect

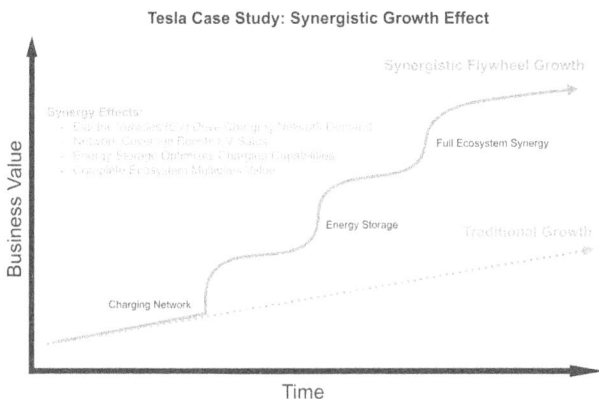

This is systems thinking taken to its highest level—engineering growth where every part of your business naturally reinforces the others while driving toward your ultimate vision.

As you start to scale these carefully selected elements of your business, you'll inevitably encounter new challenges. The landscape shifts, the rules change, and suddenly you're playing a whole new game.

"Synergistic Scaling isn't just about growing bigger.
It's about growing better."

So how do you navigate these shifting sands? How do you overcome the unique challenges that come with each stage of growth? That's exactly what we're going to explore next.

NAVIGATING THE GROWTH GAUNTLET

It could likely go without saying that scaling a business isn't a smooth, linear process. Usually quite the opposite; it's more like running a gauntlet, with each stage of growth presenting its unique set of challenges and where "the rules" seem to change at every level. Where the strategies that worked brilliantly at one revenue level might become actively harmful at the next.

Let's break down these stages and explore how to overcome their specific challenges while maintaining the integrity of your vision.

Startup Stage: $0 - $1 Million

At this stage, you're all about proving your concept and finding product-market fit. The main challenge here is focus, or rather, the lack of it. It's tempting to chase every opportunity, pivot at every setback, and try to be all things to all people.

The key to overcoming this challenge means having the courage to say *"no"* to good opportunities so you can say *"yes"* to great ones, ruthlessly prioritizing and aligning every action with your core vision.

Take Airbnb in its early days. They could have expanded into numerous travel-related services, but they maintained a laser focus on their core offering: unique places to stay. This disciplined approach allowed them to perfect their model before expanding.

Strategies for this stage:

1. Implement regular vision alignment checks.
2. Create a "not-to-do" list alongside your to-do list.
3. Seek mentors who can provide perspective and keep you accountable.

As you transition from the startup stage to the growth stage, remember that the skills and strategies that got you here won't necessarily carry you forward. It's time to shift gears and prepare for a new set of challenges.

Growth Stage: $1 Million - $10 Million

At this stage, you've proven your concept, and now you're facing the challenges of rapid growth. The main pitfall here is losing sight of your vision amidst the chaos of scaling.

Many businesses at this stage become so focused on metrics and more revenue that they forget why they started in the first place. The result is often a larger business, but one that's lost its soul.

The antidote for this is weaving your vision into every aspect of your growing operation, from hiring practices to customer service protocols to strategic planning.

Strategies for this stage:

1. Develop a robust onboarding process that immerses new hires in your vision.
2. Create feedback loops that constantly check operations against your core vision.
3. Implement systems thinking tools to map how growth in one area affects others.

As you navigate this stage, keep in mind that the complexity of your business is increasing. You're no longer wearing all the hats; you're building entire departments. This transition sets the stage for the next phase of growth.

Expansion Stage: $10 Million - $50 Million

During the expansion stage, complexity becomes your biggest challenge. Your business is no longer a speedboat that can turn on a dime—it's more like a cruise ship with multiple decks and departments.

The danger here is what I call "Vision Dilution." As you add more layers of management and expand into new markets, your original vision can get lost in translation. You might find different departments interpreting your vision in conflicting ways, leading to inconsistency and internal friction.

This is why having a clearly defined mission statement and core values is so critical. The larger a business becomes, the more imperative it is that decisions are made with a consistent ethos to maintain synergy across all departments.

Strategies for this stage:

1. Develop a detailed vision playbook that can guide decision-making at all levels.
2. Implement cross-functional teams to ensure vision alignment across departments.
3. Create a robust internal communication strategy to keep everyone connected.

Conquering the expansion stage is a huge milestone, and you should absolutely celebrate that win. But your success at this level actually sets up your next big set of challenges. Just like when you learn to surf (if you haven't tried it, you should give it a go!), as soon as you master catching the small waves, you find yourself eyeing those bigger ones out on the horizon.

I've watched visionary leaders hit this point and either get comfortable (big mistake) or get overwhelmed by what comes next. The key is to stay hungry while at the same time remaining strategic about your next moves.

Now, I know what some of you might be thinking, *Mike, these revenue numbers seem astronomical from where I'm sitting.* And you know what? That's completely fair. Every business has its own natural size and optimal scale. Some of the most profitable and impactful businesses I've worked with never crossed $10 million in revenue, and they're absolutely crushing it in their space (and enjoying their life along the way).

The numbers themselves aren't what's important here. What matters is understanding how your challenges evolve as you grow, regardless of your ultimate revenue target. The principles we're covering apply whether you're scaling to $1 million or $100 million. It's about recognizing the patterns and preparing for them before they show up at your door.

I've worked with business owners and executives across a wide range of revenue, and what I've noticed is that the leaders who build the strongest foundations at each stage are the ones who study and prepare for the next level, even if they never plan to get there. Why?

Because understanding larger-scale challenges gives you a perspective that makes you better at operating at your current level.

Think of it like a chef studying advanced culinary techniques. Even if they never plan to open a Michelin-star restaurant, that knowledge inevitably improves their current cooking. The same principle applies here.

So, as we move into discussing the established stage, I encourage you to focus less on the specific revenue numbers and more on the principles and patterns we're uncovering. These insights will serve you regardless of your ultimate destination.

Established Stage: $50 Million and Beyond

What fascinates me most about companies reaching the $50 million mark and beyond is how the challenges shift dramatically. The larger you grow, the more your biggest threats shift from external competition to internal dynamics.

Many leaders at this stage grapple with what I call "summit syndrome"—that feeling of reaching what they thought was the top, only to realize it's actually another base camp. Some of the most impactful conversations I've had with clients at this stage weren't about growth strategies or market expansion; they were about fundamentally redefining what success means for their organization and even more so for themselves personally.

Conversations I have with leaders at this stage often circle back to one crucial question: "What are we really building here?" Contrary to what most business books would tell you, scaling up isn't always the answer.

I remember sitting with the founder of a fast-growing brand in the beverage space, who had just declined an aggressive growth opportunity. His team thought he was crazy. The numbers looked fantastic on paper, but he had total clarity about his vision. "We could double our size," he told me, "but we'd destroy the legitimacy we've built amongst our core customer base." He knew exactly what his organization did best and refused to dilute that power just for the sake of being bigger.

That's what I find most compelling about advising established organizations—watching leaders wrestle with these profound questions about purpose and legacy. Some choose to sell at their peak, understanding that new leadership might be exactly what their vision needs to reach the next level. Others intentionally maintain their size, focusing instead on deepening their impact in their chosen market.

Through these conversations, I've noticed that the most fulfilled leaders share one common trait: they've *defined success on their own terms*. Not by market expectations or industry benchmarks, but by how well their organization serves its highest purpose.

This is where true systems thinking becomes absolutely critical. At this scale, you need to zoom out and see not just where your business is, but where the entire ecosystem around you is heading. Like Microsoft under Nadella's leadership—when he took over, they were still a tech giant but losing ground fast. Instead of pushing harder on their existing path, they completely reimagined how their vision would manifest in a changing world.

They made some bold moves:

- Embraced open-source (which was practically heresy at Microsoft before)
- Shifted from one-time software sales to subscription models
- Went all-in on cloud computing

But here's the key insight that most people miss: These weren't only tactical changes; they were also a complete renewal of how Microsoft saw itself and its role in the world.

The lesson here isn't that I want you to copy Microsoft's playbook. It's understanding that at the established stage, the game becomes less about growth for growth's sake and more about intentional evolution. Some of the most powerful moves you can make might actually involve getting smaller in some areas to get stronger in others.

Early in my career, I was admittedly caught up in the "bigger is better" mindset. But after years of advising businesses of all sizes, I've learned that the most impressive victories don't always show up on a balance sheet. They show up in the lives changed, the innovations sparked, and the legacies built.

This understanding has transformed how I approach these high-level strategy sessions. Now, I push my clients to wrestle with questions like:

- What would make us more effective at our mission— getting bigger or getting better?
- Are we growing because we should or because we think we must?
- How do we want our organization to be remembered?
- What kind of legacy are we really trying to build?

The answers to these questions often surprise everyone involved. I've seen organizations intentionally get smaller to increase their impact. I've watched others completely reinvent themselves while keeping their core purpose intact.

Remember this: calcification doesn't just happen in your systems and processes. It can happen in your thinking too. That's why the most dynamic organizations at this stage constantly challenge their assumptions about what "success" actually means.

Whether you're building toward an exit, scaling to new heights, or optimizing for sustained impact, the key is staying true to your own definition of success.

As we wrap up this chapter on scaling, my recommendation is to reflect on what "success" really means to you, your team, and ultimately, your customers. Growth just for the sake of being bigger and making more money isn't always the answer. While I think it's safe to say that most of us are driven to achieve more, we never want to do so by sacrificing our souls.

Like the often quoted verse in the Bible, "What good will it be for someone to gain the whole world, yet forfeit their soul?" (Matthew 16:26). This profound question reminds us that in our pursuit of growth and success, we have to be careful not to lose sight of our core values and purpose along the way.

As visionary leaders, our ultimate responsibility to our team and market is *maintaining alignment*. We'll dig into this concept further in the next chapter, as it's a term often used but can be a bit vague. What does it mean to maintain perfect alignment? What are the benefits? How do we achieve it? This is what we'll cover next.

When scaling your business, keep your vision front and center. Let it be the filter through which you make every decision and the standard against which you measure every opportunity. When you scale with vision, you're not just building a bigger business. You're building a better world.

QUESTIONS TO CONSIDER

1. Apply the Scalability DNA Test to your core operations. Which elements of your business actually become more valuable with scale versus those that just get more complex? Where are your current systems fighting growth rather than facilitating it?

2. Think about your "Infrastructure Gap." What systems in your business were built for your current size rather than your desired future? If you 10x your revenue tomorrow, which systems would break first and why?

3. Examine your last three growth initiatives. Were you building skyscrapers (isolated growth) or engineered ecosystems (synergistic growth)? How could you transform these initiatives into self-reinforcing flywheels that accelerate each other?

4. Run your vision through the Values Stress Test. At 10x your current size, which core values would be hardest to maintain? What specific systems could you build now to ensure these values actually strengthen with scale rather than dilute?

5. Looking at the Growth Gauntlet stages we covered. Where are you now, and what's your next inflection point? What behaviors or systems that served you well at your current stage might become liabilities at the next level?

NINE
THE PURPOSE-PROFIT FLYWHEEL

TOPIC: BALANCING PURPOSE AND PROFIT FOR LASTING SUCCESS

*"Every decision you make sends ripples throughout
your organization. Each ripple either reinforces
or erodes your purpose."*
—Jim Collins, *Good to Great*

BALANCING PURPOSE AND PROFIT FOR LASTING SUCCESS

You're scaling rapidly. The dream you started with is becoming reality. Your vision is taking shape, and the market is responding. This is what success looks like... right?

But something feels off...

Maybe it started subtly—a small compromise here, a "temporary" deviation from your values there. The pressure to hit quarterly targets is growing. Investors want faster growth. The board pushes for higher margins. Your team, once unified by a shared mission, now speaks primarily in terms of KPIs and profit margins.

This isn't your typical "we're losing our culture" story that most business gurus warn you about. This is deeper. More systemic. It's in the micro-decisions being made daily across your organization. The small compromises that seem logical in isolation but create massive deviation when compounded.

I see this pattern emerge so predictably that you could set your watch by it. A visionary builds something remarkable. They scale. They optimize. They implement "best practices." And somewhere in that process, the engine they built to bring their vision to life starts working against that very vision.

"The greatest threat to your vision isn't opposition—it's optimization—of the wrong things."

This problem is so sinister because it's hard to spot when each individual decision makes perfect sense. Focusing on premium users first to fund expansion? Logical. Optimizing for short-term revenue to fuel growth? Standard practice. Building systems around easily measurable metrics rather than mission impact? Practical.

That's what makes this so dangerous: These aren't failures of intention. They're failures of design. This happens when the systems built to scale a business are mistakenly engineered to prioritize what could be measured easily over what matters most.

I'll share a story that illustrates this perfectly. Nichole founded a start-up that was developing a revolutionary educational technology platform. Her mission was crystal clear from day one: make high-quality education accessible to everyone, regardless of economic status. The company was growing rapidly and attracting major investors who saw the potential for massive returns.

But with each funding round, the pressure mounted. "Just raise the prices a little," they said. "Focus on the premium market first. We can serve the underserved communities later, once we've scaled."

The suggestions seemed reasonable on paper. After all, isn't that just smart business? But the founders could feel the company's soul slipping away, one board meeting at a time.

This is the crucible that tests every visionary leader. The moment when the pure idealism that fueled your early days meets the harsh realities of scaling a business. It's easy to stay true to your purpose when you're small. But what happens when millions—or billions—of dollars are at stake? When hundreds or thousands of employees depend on your decisions? When stakeholders demand ever-increasing returns?

> *"The true test of leadership isn't maintaining your purpose when it's easy, but defending it when it could cost you everything."*

The conventional wisdom says you have to choose: either chase profits and leave your purpose behind, or stick to your mission and accept limited growth. But that's a false dichotomy. The most successful companies of our time have found ways to turn their purpose into rocket fuel for growth.

Look at Patagonia, a company that's grown into a billion-dollar enterprise not despite its environmental mission, but *because* of it. Their unwavering commitment to environmental sustainability has done more than just earn them loyal customers; it's become their greatest competitive advantage. When they launched their famous "Don't Buy This Jacket" campaign, encouraging consumers to think twice before purchasing, they stayed true to their values and created a level of brand loyalty that their competitors can only dream of.

Now, this is typically where most writers would launch into a passionate defense of "purpose over profit." But you already know purpose matters. You wouldn't still be reading this book if you didn't, and if I'm being perfectly honest, I *really* like profits. So the real question isn't whether purpose and profit should coexist—it's how to engineer systems that make their integration *inevitable* rather than oppositional.

In this chapter, we're going to do something different. Instead of philosophical arguments about the value of purpose, we're going to explore how to build systems that make purpose profitable by design. We will look at practical strategies for using your purpose-based vision and mission as a competitive advantage, while you scale at the same time. A true "both/and" approach.

Most importantly, I'm going to show you how to build systems that naturally align profit with purpose, so you're not constantly caught in the crossfire between the two. I'll start by addressing one of the most common challenges visionary leaders face: stakeholder pressure.

BEYOND MISSION STATEMENTS

Let's talk about something that many leaders struggle with, but few admit openly: What if you're not entirely clear on your purpose? What if your mission statement feels more like a corporate-fill-in-the-blank style Mad Libs than a genuine calling?

You're not alone. I can't tell you how many times I've sat across from highly successful entrepreneurs who, when asked about their purpose, recite a polished mission statement that sounds great but feels hollow. Or they stumble and say something like, "Well, we want to be the leading provider of..." *Yawn.*

Here's the truth: Your purpose isn't a marketing exercise. It's not about sounding noble or impressing anyone. And contrary to popular belief, it doesn't have to involve saving the world or solving hunger (though it certainly can if that's your calling).

> *"Your purpose is simply the deepest truth about why your business exists and the unique value you bring to the world."*

Let me share something that might be controversial: Most mission statements are garbage. They're written by a committee, designed to offend no one and inspire no one. They use words like "premier," "leading," and "world-class" as if every business can be the "leading provider" of something.

Real purpose is different. It's specific. It's honest. Sometimes it's even a bit uncomfortable because it forces you to stand for something, which means you might have to stand against something else.

Take Patagonia again. Their purpose isn't some vague commitment to "quality outdoor gear." They explicitly exist to "save our home planet." That's specific. That's polarizing. That's real.

But where many leaders get stuck is they think their purpose needs to sound charitable or altruistic to be valid. It doesn't. Your purpose just needs to be *true*.

Let me ask you some questions that might help uncover yours:

Think about what makes you angry about your industry. What's fundamentally broken that you're trying to fix? Now imagine money was no object. What would you still want your company to do? There's usually profound truth in that answer.

Listen carefully to what your most loyal customers say you do for them that goes beyond your actual product or service. They often see your purpose more clearly than you do. Then consider what would be lost in the world if your company disappeared tomorrow. Not just the products or services, but the deeper impact you have on people's lives.

These aren't just philosophical questions. Your answers are the raw material of real purpose.

I recently worked with a client who runs a successful accounting firm. When we started discussing purpose, he was apologetic. "We just do taxes," he said. "It's not exactly saving the world."

But as we began working together on it, we found something far more compelling. His firm had built a reputation for working with first-generation immigrant business owners. He was drawn to this because he remembered how his parents had struggled to navigate the financial system when they first came to America. His firm wasn't just "doing taxes"—they were helping newcomers build legitimate businesses and create generational wealth.

That's purpose. Not because it sounds good on a wall, but because it's true.

MAKING PURPOSE PROFITABLE

Growing a business is like navigating a ship through increasingly treacherous waters. With each new level of success, more voices join the conversation about which direction to sail. And let's be real—most of those voices will be pushing hard for whatever brings the fastest financial returns.

Most companies don't lose their way through conscious choices. Instead, it happens through designing systems and strategies around seemingly innocent questions like:

"What metrics should we track?"

"How should we structure incentives?"

"What should we optimize for?"

The answers seem obvious at first. Track revenue. Measure growth. Optimize for efficiency. Pretty straight forward right?! But here's what makes this tricky: These aren't wrong questions to ask. They're *incomplete* ones.

When you build systems around incomplete metrics, you get incomplete results. It's like trying to navigate using only a compass when you need GPS. The compass isn't wrong; it's just insufficient for the complexity of the modern journey.

Let's return to Nicole's story for a moment, looking at how she transformed this challenge into an opportunity. Instead of caving to investor pressure to abandon her mission of accessible education, she completely reframed the conversation. She brought data showing how their mission-aligned approach was actually creating a competitive moat that others couldn't easily replicate.

Those deep relationships they'd built with underserved communities? They weren't just fulfilling their purpose—they were building invaluable trust and brand loyalty that would pay dividends for years to come. The company's commitment to accessibility was a noble goal that was driving innovation in ways their competitors couldn't match.

"In a well-designed business, purpose isn't a cost center—it's your most powerful profit driver."

This is where systems thinking becomes crucial. Most companies make the mistake of treating purpose and profit as opposing forces that need to be balanced. But what if you could build systems where pursuing your purpose naturally drives profit, and vice versa?

The key is shifting the conversation from short-term tradeoffs to long-term value creation. Here's how you make that happen:

First, you need to get serious about tracking the full spectrum of value your purpose-driven initiatives create. I know what many of you are thinking, "Mike, I already track everything." But here's what I've found working with countless companies: most are only measuring direct financial returns, completely missing the goldmine of secondary effects.

Recent studies by global management consulting firm McKinsey & Company revealed that purpose-driven companies are outperforming their peers across every meaningful metric. Higher customer loyalty. Stronger employee engagement. Better innovation. Lower acquisition costs. Higher lifetime value. This isn't just feel-good stuff; it's a concrete business advantage.

The challenge is making these connections visible to stakeholders. Think of it like installing floodlights on a dark path—you're not changing the path, you're just making it visible. One of my past clients built what they called a "Purpose-Profit Dashboard." It wasn't anything fancy—just a simple system tracking how their community initiatives were directly impacting customer retention rates. But it transformed their board meetings. Suddenly, their purpose-driven programs weren't seen as cost centers anymore; they were recognized as profit drivers.

When you're ready to build your dashboard, start by identifying three to four key metrics that show the direct connection between your purpose-driven activities and business results. The key is to draw clear, undeniable lines between purpose and profit.

BUILDING SYSTEMS THAT NATURALLY ALIGN PURPOSE AND PROFIT

Alright, as promised, it's time we tackle one of the biggest myths in business: the idea that you need to constantly choose between purpose and profit. This mindset is so pervasive that organizations actually design their structures in ways that guarantee conflict between these two forces. It's like building a house with fundamental structural flaws and then wondering why the walls keep cracking.

According to Harvard Business Review, companies that treat purpose and profit as integrated rather than competing priorities are 2.5x more likely to be high-performing organizations. Yet, surprisingly, 67% of leaders report struggling to create this integration at a systems level.

Think of your business systems like a network of rivers. Traditional setups have purpose flowing one way and profit flowing another, occasionally meeting at conflict points. We want to create a system where these streams merge into a single, powerful flow.

Sounds good, right? But how do you start redirecting these streams?

First, redesign your decision-making frameworks. Most companies have separate tracks for "mission decisions" and "business decisions." Instead, create frameworks that evaluate both purpose and profit simultaneously. When evaluating new opportunities, don't just run the numbers. Score each opportunity on both financial potential and mission alignment.

This does not have to be as complicated as you may initially think. Let me give you a practical example of how this works. James runs a commercial construction company in Texas that transformed its business by integrating environmental sustainability into its core operations. Instead of treating sustainability as a separate initiative or cost center, they made it central to their business model.

Here's how their purpose-profit flywheel began spinning:

- They started by tracking and optimizing material waste on job sites
- Reduced waste led to lower material costs
- Lower costs enabled more competitive bidding
- More competitive bids won more contracts
- Higher volume created leverage with suppliers

- Supplier leverage enabled bulk purchasing of sustainable materials
- Sustainable practices attracted premium clients
- Premium clients provided higher margins
- Higher margins funded more sustainable innovations

Within 15 months, they had become the go-to contractor for environmentally conscious commercial projects in their region. Their waste reduction initiatives alone saved over $2M annually. But here's the best part: *none of this required radical changes*. They simply started measuring and optimizing what they were already doing but through a different lens.

THE POWER OF PURPOSEFUL INTEGRATION

Now, some of you might be thinking, *This all sounds great in theory, Mike, but in the real world, there are always going to be tradeoffs between purpose and profit.*

You're right—there will be tradeoffs. But most of these tradeoffs exist because of how we've designed our businesses, not because they're inevitable.

Think of it like a car engine. Early engines had to trade off between power and fuel efficiency. But as engineering evolved, we learned to design engines that could deliver both more efficiently. Modern businesses are no different. With the right systems in place, purpose and profit don't just coexist—they amplify each other.

"The most successful companies of the future will be the ones that figure out how to turn purpose into profit."

Don't overcomplicate this. Start small. Pick one department or team to pilot these changes, gather data on what works, and then scale what's successful across your organization.

Powerful things happen when these systems start working together. Suddenly, you're not constantly mediating between purpose and profit. They're working in harmony, reinforcing each other, creating a perpetual motion machine that drives both impact and growth.

Remember the three key challenges we discussed:

- Managing stakeholder pressure for faster growth
- Measuring the true ROI of purpose-driven initiatives
- Building systems that naturally align purpose and profit

Mastering these elements means you'll have a business where doing good and doing well aren't competing priorities but complementary forces.

The data is clear: Companies that successfully integrate purpose and profit outperform their peers by virtually every metric.[1] They're more innovative, more resilient, and more profitable over the long term. But most importantly, they're built to last. In a world where change is the only constant, these companies have something invaluable: a North Star that guides their evolution while keeping them true to their core.

I've developed a Purpose-Profit Flywheel™ template to simplify this alignment process. You can download it for free at SystemsThink ingVisionary.com/resources. Use this framework as a diagnostic tool to identify areas where you can strengthen the alignment between purpose and profit in your organization.

---

1. Gunnar Friede, Timo Busch, and Alexander Bassen, "ESG and Financial Performance: Aggregated Evidence from More Than 2000 Empirical Studies," *Journal of Sustainable Finance & Investment* 5, no. 4 (2015): 210–233 https://www.tandfonline.com/doi/full/10.1080/20430795.2015.1118917.

Purpose Profit Flywheel™

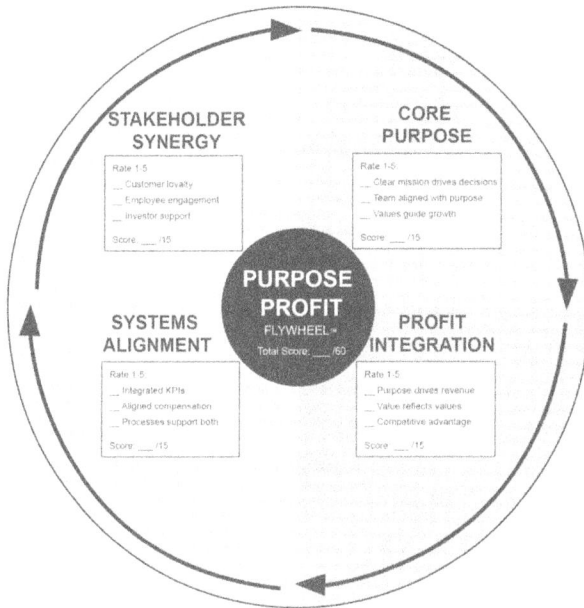

The Purpose-Profit Flywheel™ is more of a navigation system than just a simple diagnostic tool.

Rate each element on a scale of 1-5, with 1 indicating significant misalignment and 5 representing perfect harmony. Total your scores across all four quadrants for a comprehensive assessment out of 60 possible points.

This score will highlight specific opportunities for growth. Where you score lowest is where your greatest leverage exists. For example, if your Core Purpose score lags, focus there first as it's the foundation everything else builds upon. If Systems Alignment needs work, that becomes your focus point. The beauty of this flywheel is that improvements in any quadrant naturally strengthen the others, creating momentum that accelerates over time. Reassess quarterly to track your progress, celebrate wins, and identify your next strategic priority. Note that even a five-point improvement can create ripple effects throughout your entire organization.

A complete scoring guide is provided with the downloadable template.

QUESTIONS TO CONSIDER

1. Strip away the PR ("public relations") version of your mission statement and get brutally honest: What would truly be lost if your company disappeared tomorrow? How explicitly are you designing your systems to amplify that unique value rather than just preserve it?

2. Audit your metrics through the Purpose-Profit Flywheel framework we covered. Which of your "purpose-driven" initiatives are creating measurable competitive advantages? Where are you treating purpose as a cost center rather than a profit driver?

3. Think about your most recent board meeting or stakeholder presentation. How did you demonstrate the connection between purpose and profit? What secondary effects and long-term value creation metrics could you start tracking to make this connection undeniable?

4. Examine your decision-making frameworks. Do they force artificial choices between purpose and profit, or are they designed to optimize for both simultaneously? What specific systems could you implement to make purpose-aligned decisions the default rather than the exception?

5. Look at your last three major strategic pivots. Were they driven by market pressure or mission alignment? How could you redesign your systems so that staying true to

your purpose becomes your strongest path to profitability?

In our final chapter, we'll integrate all the elements of systems thinking, visionary leadership, and purpose-driven growth into a cohesive whole. I'll share concrete frameworks you can implement immediately to create lasting transformation throughout your organization.

Purpose and profit don't have to be opposing forces in your business. The visionaries who truly make history design organizations where these elements naturally strengthen each other. When you engineer your systems correctly, purpose becomes your ultimate competitive advantage - the cornerstone of an unstoppable organization.

TEN
PUTTING IT ALL TOGETHER
TOPIC: BRINGING YOUR VISION TO LIFE

*"You can't fake commitment. Either you have it, or you don't.
And when you do, it shows in everything you do."*
—John C. Maxwell, *The 21 Irrefutable Laws of Leadership*

BRINGING YOUR VISION TO LIFE

Have you ever felt that electric surge just before launching something transformational? That moment when your vision is crystal clear, but you get that feeling in your gut reminding you that once you begin, there's no turning back? It's thrilling, a little terrifying, and exactly where I hope this chapter finds you.

Throughout this book, we've dissected what it truly means to be a Systems-Thinking Visionary: someone who transforms bold ideas into executable strategies, combines creative vision with disciplined implementation, and scales with integrity. This final chapter serves as your integration point—where theory meets application. It's time to synthesize these powerful concepts into a unified framework that propels you forward. Consider this your launchpad for decisive action and extraordinary results.

To do that, you'll need a tool that bridges the gap between theory and practice and transforms disconnected elements into a cohesive, actionable framework. That tool is **The Visionary Integration Matrix™**, and it will change the way you lead.

Let's shift into full-on integration mode.

THE VISIONARY INTEGRATION MATRIX™: YOUR BLUEPRINT FOR ALIGNMENT

Over the years, I've noticed that it's really common for visionary leaders to excel in individual areas—crafting bold ideas, coming up with competition-killing strategies, inspiring their teams—but then struggling to connect these elements into a seamless whole. It's like having all the ingredients for a gourmet dish but no recipe to bring them together.

The **Visionary Integration Matrix™** is your recipe. Think of it as your organizational GPS, a tool that helps you assess your current position, align your efforts, and map the path forward across three essential dimensions:

1. **Vision**—Your ability to articulate a compelling future and inspire action.
2. **Systems**—The processes that make execution scalable and efficient.
3. **Implementation**—The discipline to translate ideas into measurable results.

When these three dimensions work together, greatness happens. The Matrix doesn't just measure where you stand; it shows you how to bring these dimensions into alignment, turning complexity into clarity and potential into performance.

If you haven't already, download a copy at SystemsThinkingVi sionary.com/resources. This is a tool you'll want to be able to access and implement more than once, so make it an easy-to-find asset.

Visionary Integration Matrix™

	LEVEL 1	LEVEL 2	LEVEL 3	LEVEL 4
VISION	Purpose unclear or inconsistently communicated	Purpose defined but not fully embedded into operations	Purpose guides most decisions and is well understood	Purpose drives all aspects of business and culture
SYSTEMS	Ad hoc processes, minimal infrastructure	Basic systems in place but not fully integrated	Integrated systems supporting most key functions	Optimized systems driving scalable growth
IMPLEMENTATION	Inconsistent execution with frequent delays	Some ideas executed but implementation often struggles	Reliable execution with occasional challenges	Consistent, rapid implementation of new initiatives

How to Use This Assessment:

1. Rate your organization on each dimension
2. Focus improvement efforts on your lowest scoring dimension
3. Perfect integration = Level 4 across all three dimensions
4. Assess each quarter to track progress

BRINGING THE MATRIX TO LIFE

To see the Matrix in action, let me tell you about Daniel, a client who's built a mobile app within the blockchain technology sector. When he and I first met, his company was already growing fast, but the cracks were definitely starting to show. "I feel like I'm drowning in complexity," he told me. "We have all these processes and people, but they're not all connected to our vision. It's like trying to coach a soccer team when everyone's running their own route."

That's where the **Visionary Integration Matrix™** comes in. Think of it as a high-resolution map of your organization that can illustrate your team's titles and position within the organization and also how their current skill sets and efficiencies collaboratively sync together.

I had Daniel and his team assess their scores across Vision, Systems, and Implementation on a scale of 1 to 4. The results were immediately eye-opening to say the least. Sales and Marketing excelled in Vision but lagged in Systems. Operations nailed Implementation but struggled to connect to the company's bigger picture.

By consolidating these scores, Daniel finally saw the full picture. He understood where his company stood and how the departments' strengths and weaknesses impacted each other. Here's the best part: the Matrix didn't just diagnose the issues; it gave him a clear path to fix them.

MASTERING THE MATRIX

Below is a step-by-step breakdown of how to use the **Visionary Integration Matrix™** to create alignment and unlock your organization's full potential:

Step 1: Assess Your Current State

Start by having each department head refer to the Matrix to score their team across Vision, Systems, and Implementation. Be brutally honest—this process only works if you're willing to confront uncomfortable truths.

Ask:

- Vision: How clearly is our purpose being communicated and understood?

- Systems: Are our processes scalable and effective, or do they create bottlenecks?

- Implementation: Are we consistently turning ideas into results?

Step 2: Identify Misalignments

Once you've gathered your scores, look for patterns. Misalignments often reveal friction points. For example:

- A strong Vision with weak Systems leads to unfulfilled potential.

- Robust Systems without strong Implementation creates paralysis by analysis.

- High Implementation without a clear Vision results in wasted effort.

Step 3: Create an Action Plan

Use the Matrix to prioritize your efforts. Focus on:

- Strengthening areas scoring at Level 1 (these are your critical vulnerabilities).
- Leveraging strengths in one department to support weaknesses in another.

For example, we discovered Daniel's HR department scored low on Systems, creating operational friction throughout the organization. By strengthening this single weak point, he triggered cascading improvements across multiple departments, amplifying overall performance company-wide.

Step 4: Embed the Matrix Into Your Culture

The **Visionary Integration Matrix™** isn't a one-and-done exercise; revisit it regularly. Schedule quarterly assessments to track progress and keep alignment front and center.

When you embed the Matrix into your organization's DNA, it becomes a shared language. Teams start thinking holistically, connecting their work to the bigger picture, and collaborating in ways that amplify results.

THE PATH FORWARD

As we bring this journey to a close, I want you to take a moment to reflect on all the ground we've covered together. You've explored what it truly means to be a Systems-Thinking Visionary. You've demystified the concept of systems, tackled the challenges of scaling, and discovered how to balance purpose and profit. And now, you have the tools to bring it all together.

Let's confront the uncomfortable truth: knowledge without implementation is just entertainment. The frameworks in these pages hold immense power, but only when activated through decisive action.

The models and frameworks we've discussed throughout this book serve as the bridge between where you are and where you're destined to be. The Visionary Integration Matrix™ is your compass for this journey.

Share these insights with your leadership team. Schedule implementation sessions. Create accountability structures. Transform these concepts from ideas on paper into operational reality in your business.

You've invested time in these pages because you're committed to building something remarkable. Now convert that commitment into momentum. The differentiator between visionaries who make history and those who merely dream isn't intelligence or luck—it's execution.

The seeds have been planted. The blueprint drawn. The decision to build rests solely with you.

Go create your masterpiece.

SuperPowers of the Systems-Thinking Visionary

- **V**ision (see compelling futures and inspire action)
- **I**mplementation (power to turn ideas into reality)
- **S**ystems (capacity to build and scale operations)
- **I**ntegration (skill at unifying all elements into a cohesive whole)
- **O**ptimization (drive to continuously improve and refine)
- **N**avigation (ability to adapt and course-correct toward your goals)

THE FINAL PAGE: A VISIONARY'S JOURNEY

As the early morning light began to spread across ancient Athens, the city stirred with activity. Among the impressive structures and winding streets stood Socrates, the philosopher renowned for his ability to illuminate complex ideas.

A young leader, Demetrius, newly tasked with a major construction project, approached Socrates. His eyes were bright with excitement but tinged with uncertainty. "How can I ensure my grand vision becomes reality and stands the test of time?" he asked, his voice carrying both ambition and apprehension.

Socrates surveyed the city's remarkable buildings, his gaze lingering on the Acropolis. "Take a good look at these structures, Demetrius. They weren't built with mere stone and mortar; they were created with clear purpose and unwavering principles."

Demetrius listened intently, his gaze following Socrates' outstretched hand. "But how do I manage such a monumental task?" he asked.

Socrates smiled, recognizing the familiar struggle of a visionary grappling with execution. "The Parthenon," he continued, gesturing to the magnificent temple, "isn't impressive solely because of its grandeur. It's the harmony between dream and reality that makes it stand out. True greatness lies in uniting lofty ideals with the minutiae of creation."

As they walked, they passed a group of craftsmen working on a new building. Socrates paused, observing their coordinated efforts. "See how each worker knows their role, yet understands the bigger picture? This is the essence of true leadership. Your task is not just to build but to orchestrate a symphony where every player contributes to the whole."

Demetrius nodded slowly, beginning to see his project in a new light. "So, I must be both dreamer and doer?"

"Indeed," Socrates affirmed. "You must hold the grand vision in your mind while rolling up your sleeves each day to bring it to life."

As the sun's rays cast a golden glow over the city, they reached a vantage point overlooking Athens. Socrates turned to Demetrius, his eyes reflecting the wisdom of ages. "Your vision, young leader, needs more than mere imagination. It requires the patience of a farmer, the precision of a sculptor, and the strategic thinking of a chess master. Your true legacy will be defined not by your dreams alone, but by how you nurture them into reality."

Demetrius stood silent for a moment, absorbing the profound insight. Then, with renewed determination, he asked, "Where do I begin?"

Socrates smiled, pleased by the young leader's eagerness. "Start by understanding the heart of your project. What is its true purpose? How does it serve the city and its people? Remember, in the grand tapestry of life, every thread affects the whole pattern. Your job is to weave your vision into the very fabric of Athens itself."

As they began their descent back into the city, Socrates added, "And never forget, Demetrius, that the path of a true leader is one of constant growth. The journey to realizing a vision is rarely a straight line. You must be as flexible as a reed in the wind, yet as committed to your purpose as the mountains are to the sky."

Demetrius nodded, feeling a new sense of clarity and confidence. As they parted ways, Socrates left him with one final thought: "Embrace your vision, build with wisdom, and leave a legacy that will echo through the ages. The future is yours to shape, young leader. Now go out there and create your masterpiece."

As Demetrius walked away, the first rays of sunlight lit up the Acropolis, bathing the city in the promise of a new day—a fitting symbol for the dawn of his own transformative journey.

"Embrace your vision.
Build with precision.
Leave a legacy."
–Michael Graham Walker

ABOUT THE AUTHOR

Michael Graham Walker has become known in many circles as the go-to Strategic Advisor for Elite Entrepreneurs. Having built and scaled multiple businesses across diverse industries, his background positions him as a vetted and reliable force in business strategy who helps transform how visionary leaders approach scale and growth. As a partner at The Wealthy Consultant and Founder and CEO of ClientBloomAi and BrightLink Consulting, Michael has spent over two decades decoding the complex relationship between visionary thinking and operational excellence.

His methodologies draw insights from a wide field of interests and study, including quantum physics, advanced systems theory, and real-world business experience, to help leaders build enterprises that scale without losing their soul in the process. His first book, *The Exceptional Experience: Building a Business Your Customers Will Love,* became an Amazon bestseller by challenging conventional wisdom about customer relationships and business growth. Now, in *The Systems-Thinking Visionary*, he reveals the frameworks and strategies that have helped hundreds of visionary leaders turn bold dreams into operational reality.

Through his work with clients, he's developed proprietary frameworks, including the Power Grid Framework™ and Visionary Integration Matrix™, which have the power to revolutionize how businesses approach scaling and sustainable growth. His message resonates with entrepreneurs and executives who refuse to choose between purpose and profit, vision and execution, or impact and scale.

Michael's work represents more than just business strategy—it's a complete reimagining of what's possible when visionary thinking meets systems excellence.

Connect on Social:
instagram.com/michaelgrahamwalker
facebook.com/michaelgrahamwalker
linkedin.com/in/michaelgrahamwalker